# in retreat

## The Canadian Forces in the Trudeau Years

## Gerald Porter

Deneau & Greenberg

**ISBN:** 0-88879-007-4
©Deneau and Greenberg Publishers Ltd.
Printed in Canada

To Phyllis, for everything . . .

And to the men and women of
the Canadian Armed Forces,
past and present, who struggled
ceaselessly in the defence of
their country during the trying
Trudeau years. Many are struggling
still.

# CONTENTS

# PREFACE

Prime Minister Pierre Trudeau is one of the most formidable opponents ever to face the Canadian Armed Forces and they are losing a silent battle which has raged since he swept to power in 1968.

Trudeau arrived at the summit of Canadian politics just months after the Pearson government had completed its controversial unification of the three traditional services. Defence Minister Paul Hellyer had merged the army, navy and air force into a single service, stripped away many of their cherished traditions and forced them into a despised green uniform.

The unhappy ranks were still reeling when Trudeau appeared. Within eighteen months he threw them into greater confusion by suddenly turning Canada's defence priorities upside down, replacing international peacekeeping with protection of national sovereignty. Where or what the threat to Canada was, he did not say.

He angered allies by suddenly pulling crack Canadian troops out of NATO's front line in Europe, although across the Iron Curtain, Soviet sabre-rattling was growing louder.

He froze the defence budget, slashed the already reduced forces by another 25,000 men and imposed an unrealistic version of bilingualism on the remainder, creating two hostile linguistic camps in the ranks of the nation's defenders.

Throughout the seventies defence policy was inconsistent and its direction confused. Six junior ministers held the defence portfolio in nine years. Defence spending plunged to a postwar low, yet the military's jobs were steadily increased.

Internally the forces' administrative gears began to slow and their over-all efficiency diminished as short-sighted personnel policies and lack of funds made it increasingly difficult to achieve the government's policy goals.

Today, after a decade of Trudeau's mismanagement of Canada's defence establishment, the forces are tired, poorly equipped and struggling to carry out their assigned tasks. They are too weak to maintain basic peacetime surveillance and control of Canadian sovereignty — their principal mission — or to play a respectable role with NATO in the collective defence of the West.

During the Trudeau years the forces' strength plunged from 104,000 to 78,000 men, the lowest number in more than twenty-five years. The number of ships, planes and other essential pieces of military hardware also declined drastically as a result of unrealistic financial restraints which made it impossible to buy replacements. Defence coffers were bled dry to pay for other government priorities.

Canadian servicemen are now flying and sailing some of the oldest military machinery in the world and the taxpayer faces a staggering multi-billion dollar bill to replace it.

Since 1969 the fundamental balance for good defence — that resources should equal commitments -- has been tipping the wrong way and it is still falling at an alarming speed. Only now is the government moving to correct the balance but many experts believe it may already be too late to restore Canada's spent forces.

Unless present defence plans change, Canada's forces of the future will be little more than skeletons in armour. This is the story of how Pierre Trudeau scuttled his own armed forces.

# ACKNOWLEDGEMENTS

This work owes its life to many people: To professors Stuart Adam and Joseph Scanlon of Carleton University's School of Journalism, where I laboured mightily and profited by it. To professor and working journalist Anthony Westell — for without his patience and direction as my thesis supervisor the orginal version of *In Retreat* might still be marching in circles. To my wife Phyllis who agonized with me through a long winter of research, doubts and writing; may she never have to hear military jargon again. And to Mrs. Anita Vandersande of Carleton, whose advice and encouragement helped me to see this project through to the end.

Finally, a special debt of gratitude is owed to those many persons associated with the armed forces who consented to interviews or offered advice which gave me a better understanding of Canadian defence problems. As a journalist I have attempted to shed light on a little known problem which affects this country's security. As a Canadian I wanted to tell my fellow countrymen why their once-proud armed forces — loyal in peacetime and steadfast in times of war — are rapidly becoming an endangered species. I hope that I might help them before it is too late.

# 1 A DECADE OF CONFUSION

The Trudeau decade has been a difficult one for Canada's military personnel. After the shock of unification had worn off, they believed service life would return to its orderly peacetime pace. But Trudeau made life in the forces more confusing and disruptive as reorganization and counter-reorganization became the rule instead of the exception. Nobody seemed to know what was going on, least of all Trudeau. The troops were marching in a fog without a map or a compass, the commander in the distance shouting orders and counter-orders, changing direction as often as the wind. By the time the rear guard had caught up, they were out of step again or going in the wrong direction.

Did Trudeau know where he was going? After several tiresome years of marching in circles his own generals concluded he did not. Worse, the troops sensed that their own leader did not much care about them, no matter how hard or how long they worked to get the job done. Morale in the forces has become a serious problem, one which gets worse with each reorganization or policy shift.

Trudeau's defence policies have been paradoxical, much like the man himself. He is an avowed pacifist, yet he did not hesitate to call the Army into the streets during the October Crisis of 1970.

His famous "just watch me" reply when asked how far he was prepared to go to maintain law and order under the War Measures Act showed he understood — and was prepared to use — military power to preserve the peace, regardless of his personal convictions. In an attempt to understand why Trudeau has run the forces down to their present emaciated state, it is worth examining where the military fits within his political vision and how that vision has manifested itself in defence policies and government priorities.

Throughout his tenure in the East Block, Trudeau has shown a strange misunderstanding, some say contempt, for Canada's armed forces. Few people would suggest that war is ever desirable, yet most realize there comes a time when a nation must defend itself against blind aggression or perish. Trudeau apparently failed to make such a distinction during the Second World War. He did not "join up" like many other young men of his age, preferring instead to continue his university education. During the 1968 leadership campaign he explained that, like many other Quebeckers, he had been taught to "keep away from imperialisitic wars."[1]

It is Trudeau's apparent misunderstanding about the true nature of the Second World War and the Allies' life and death struggle against Nazi Germany which leaves his own generals puzzled. They believe that he either does not understand the role of the military in a free society or just does not like them. In any event, they continue to view each other coolly from a distance.

One of Trudeau's first initiatives after taking power was to call for a fresh look at Canada's foreign policy. This exercise produced the so-called Third Option. It pulled Canada away from its traditional postwar alignment with the U.S. on international matters and set in motion policies which would eventually emasculate the armed forces. The radical new policy featured an association with Europe and Japan and diplomatic relations with Russia and China, and envisioned helping the impoverished nations of the Third World to build a new economic order. This was to be achieved by "pursuing national aims and interests in the international environment. It is the extension abroad of national policies."[2] Canada's domestic and foreign policies were directed to the common goal of creating a new international society based on a greater sharing of resources. Trudeau had long believed that hunger was a greater threat to world peace than the arms race, so Canada would contribute bread, butter and technology to the hungry instead of bullets. Having framed a new (and controversial) foreign policy objective for Canada, Trudeau then tailored his armed forces accordingly.

Trudeau's thinking on these matters was most explicitly expressed on May 26, 1978, when he made his first speech as Prime Minister to the United Nations. Addressing the General Assembly's special session on disarmament, Trudeau outlined a Canadian plan for slowing the nuclear arms race and nurturing development of a new economic order.

Under the plan, nuclear nations would be asked to begin cutting back defence spending on new strategic nuclear weapons systems. The money saved would be deposited in a special Third World development fund. Nuclear nations that would not play would be fined and the money put into the fund. Trudeau also stressed the contribution made to world disarmament by his government, noting that Canada was "the first nuclear arms country to have chosen to divest itself of nuclear weapons."[3]

Trudeau's personal commitment to disarmament is commendable but to many observers, including leading newspapers on both sides of the Atlantic, it appeared naive and hypocritical in light of trends behind the Iron Curtain. In recent years the Soviet Union and its Warsaw Pact allies have built the most powerful military machine in the world and there is no indication they have any intention of slowing down. After Trudeau's speech to the UN, both the *Washington Post* and London's *Sunday Express* summed up growing criticism of Trudeau's hypocritical position on collective defence by noting that it was easy for Canada to embark on a road of unilateral disarmament while huddled securely under the U.S. nuclear umbrella. Europeans, who were nervously watching the growing Soviet military threat on their borders, could afford no such moral luxury.[4] Why did Trudeau neglect his own forces at a time when concerned NATO planners were urging members to bolster their military commitments to the Alliance?

The answer appears to be two-fold: First, because Trudeau naively believed the Communists posed no threat to the West, despite tragic evidence to the contrary; and second, because he believed it was better for Canada to flow with the already-marching "caravan of humanity . . . towards the Left"[5] rather than resist or be engulfed by it. If no threat existed and the leftward march was inevitable, Canada had no need for expensive armed forces. Thus, he could justifiably divert monies from defence to finance his other priorities, such as bilingualism and international aid.

Unfortunately for Canada and its armed forces, Trudeau's foreign and defence policies have been based on a mistaken assumption that Soviet communism was, as he claimed, involved in "a slow evolution toward more liberal communism,"[6] so Canada could afford to drop its guard in dealing with Communist nations. As political analyst Philip C. Bom notes in his book *Trudeau — Truth and Consequences:* "Trudeau's (foreign policy) priority was based on his view of reality, namely, that there was no Communist threat."[7] Fearing no aggression, he then pursued a positive policy of friendship with the Soviet Union and its Warsaw Pact allies.

Détente requires trust and from the very beginning that is what Trudeau evidently had in the Russians. Despite the Soviet invasion of Czechoslovakia and subsequent military build-up, Trudeau shocked NATO allies by suddenly pulling most of his best troops out of Germany on the eve of disarmament talks, forcing others to fill the breach and weakening the West's bargaining hand.

In the past few years U.S. President Jimmy Carter and other western leaders have publicly denounced the Kremlin for failing to abide by the spirit of détente, calling for greater freedom for Soviet citizens. They appear to have heard the warnings of such respected Soviet exiles as Alexander Solzhenitsyn that détente is a smokescreen for the creation of a military juggernaut bent on bringing the West to its knees and have started beefing up their armed forces. "Nuclear war is not even necessary to the Soviet Union," Solzhenitsyn told the West in 1976, "you can be taken simply with bare hands...Now it is the Soviet Union that has the navy, controls the seas and has the bases. You may call this détente as you like, but after Angola I just can't understand how one's tongue can utter the word."[8] But in Canada, although men like Alexei Myagkov (*Inside the KGB,* 1976) warned that détente was used for espionage, Trudeau has been determined to pursue the spirit of détente while allowing his armed forces to wither away. The Soviets have done exactly the opposite.

NATO planners now predict the mighty armies of the Warsaw Pact could take Europe by force of arms, with or without nuclear weapons, in a surprise attack, in about thirty-six to forty-eight hours.[9] In less than a decade the Soviet Union has put its economy on a wartime footing, spending more than 10 percent of its gross national product (GNP) on defence. NATO also fears that unless alliance members continue to counterbalance the growing Soviet military might — demonstrate the will to resist through a tougher military stance — western Europe could fall to the Soviets, piece by piece, without a shot being fired.

The translation of Trudeau's foreign policy assumptions into defence policy took place rapidly on his becoming Prime Minister. Less than six months after taking office he began to cut down the forces. In the Fall of 1968, he ordered an across-the-board cut in staff for all government departments. Defence was given no credit for what Hellyer had already lopped off and its strength was cut back within two years to 94,000—6,000 below what Hellyer considered to be the acceptable minimum. Recruitment was choked to a trickle and a major defence review ordered.

On April 3 1969, Trudeau announced major changes in defence policy which gave the forces a dim outline of the future. Canada would remain a partner in its two collective defence pacts, NATO and NORAD (North American Air Defence Command), but the number of troops in Europe would be reduced. The most significant change was Trudeau's reversal of defence priorities, promoting the protection of national sovereignty to top of the list, while NATO and peacekeeping, the forces' principal missions for two decades, were pushed to the bottom. This strange new order upset many of Canada's allies who believed the new priorities signalled Trudeau's intention to eventually withdraw from NATO, weakening the already waning strength of the West's major shield against growing Soviet might. In conjunction with Trudeau's new foreign policy, it appeared Canada was trying to build a bridge to the Third World by burning the old one to friendly allies, long cemented by mutual defence pacts. The new priorities were: (1) surveillance of Canadian territory and coastlines to protect sovereignty; (2) defence of North America in cooperation with U.S. forces; (3) NATO commitments; (4) international peacekeeping.

On September 19, 1969, Defence Minister Leo Cadieux announced how Trudeau's policies were to be implemented. Canada's 10,000-man front line NATO force in Europe would be cut in half, deprived of its nuclear weapons and retired to a reserve position. At home, manpower would be reduced to 82,000 by 1972, a number of famous English-speaking regiments disbanded to make way for new French-speaking units, and the defence budget frozen at $1.8 billion for three years. Trudeau had decided to cut the NATO troop commitment because he claimed a Europe risen from the ashes of war could afford to pay more for its own defence and because he needed money to pay for other priorities. His military experts had told him it would cost $2.5 billion a year to continue all existing defence programs.[10]

Cadieux also announced that the forces of the future would be less warlike and engaged more in national development roles. These had not yet been defined but they included increased use of soldiers in road building, northern projects and international aid schemes.

In August 1971, the Trudeau government issued its first and only White Paper on defence policy. *Defence in the 70s*[11] confirmed the new defence priorities but it did not elaborate on how the forces would carry them out. The paper was more a philosophical treatise on defence matters than an assessment of capability.

The paper stated that a catastrophic war between Russia and the United States constituted the only major threat to Canada, which unfortunately happened to be in the middle geographically. Canada's overriding defence objective was, therefore, the prevention of nuclear war by promoting peaceful solutions to world problems and by contributing to the system of stable mutual deterrence through collective defence arrangements. In reality, the intent was to secure Canada's survival by helping to protect the U.S. nuclear deterrent—the continental United States itself, the West's major arsenal and nuclear check on itchy Russian trigger fingers. Conventional strategic wisdom dictated that as long as America was strong and well defended, the Russians would not chance a limited nuclear war in Europe for fear of swift and massive retaliation from U.S.-based nuclear missiles.

The Canadian forces' principal role, however, did not reflect the conclusions of the White Paper. It remained the protection of national sovereignty, with increased emphasis on control and presence in the North. An important yet puzzling point to emerge was the doctrine of "compatibility." In future, the forces would be engaged in an increasing number of national development roles, so major equipment purchased would have to be compatible with domestic needs. As a result, the NATO army would be re-equipped with light armoured vehicles instead of main battle tanks, because tanks were not required in Canada, although they were the principal piece of conventional weaponry used by Warsaw Pact forces.

In 1973, responding to rising nationalist pressure, the government balked at renewing the old NORAD agreement in force since 1958. Under the pact, Americans controlled much of Canada's airspace and some nationalists saw it as a dangerous infringement of sovereignty. In May 1975, Canada renewed its NORAD membership for a further five years, but with a difference. In the early 1980s, NORAD boundaries are to be redrawn along national lines and Canada will assume command and control of its own airspace.

When the forces came out of the three-year budget freeze in mid-1974, they brought with them an inventory of antique equipment with which to meet their growing responsibilities. To find a solution to the problem, Cabinet launched the Defence Structure Review in November 1974. Its purpose was, according to an internal memo, "to provide an agreed framework for the future structuring of the Canadian Forces and the Department of National Defence, in order to achieve the objectives of the government's defence policy and at the same time provide financial stability for the planning and operation of the defence program over the next five years."[12] In short, to review tasks and identify the resources the forces would need to carry them out.

A year later, on November 27, 1975, Defence Minister James Richardson announced the results of the first two parts of the review. Defence priorities remained the same, but the government clarified its murky position on NATO by agreeing to re-equip its small army in Germany with tanks instead of light armour. Long-range patrol aircraft would be bought to increase surveillance of the North and coastal areas and studies were planned to find replacements for old ships and fighter aircraft. These are currently underway, along with studies to identify the infrastructure required to support the forces of the future.

In the past few years the government has shown a renewed interest in NATO and collective security and less in promoting the virtues of the sovereignty protection role, a role which has never been satisfactorily defined. Much of the renewed interest in NATO is a result of Trudeau's desire to increase trans-Atlantic trade with Europe but some is in response to American and European pressure on Canada to start shouldering a fair share of the collective defence burden.

Trudeau's inconsistent defence policies also played havoc with the defence budget. Because military planners never knew for certain how much money they would get the next year, or in what direction defence policy would swing, it became virtually impossible to make long-range spending goals for equipment acquisition and devise a financial formula to achieve them.

Hellyer had frozen the defence budget in 1964 at about $1.5 billion a year for five years and had launched a $1.5 billion re-equipment program that was almost complete when Trudeau took power. The program had produced new ships, aircraft and light armour but more equipment was urgently required. The second five-year plan, scheduled to start in 1969-70, would have produced tanks for the Army, a long-range patrol plane for the Navy, and new fighters for the Air Force. But the three-year freeze on defence spending at $1.8 billion stalled these projects. In addition, much of the new equipment that was rolling in became surplus to requirement because of the new defence priorities.

Hellyer had also cut personnel and administrative costs with the aim of devoting 25 percent of defence spending to the purchase and upkeep of capital equipment—weapons, rolling stock and major construction. By the time he left defence in 1968, he had raised the share spent on capital goods from 12 percent to about 16 percent, the highest figure in a decade. The Trudeau freeze changed all that.

Between 1969 and 1973, inflation cut the purchasing power of the frozen budget by more than 15 percent. Thus the predicted savings from the manpower reduction program did not appear. By mid-1973, the portion of the budget devoted to capital expenditure had plunged to an all-time low of 9 percent and it appeared that soaring personnel costs would drive it down still more.

On October 10, 1973, Richardson announced the details of the first post-freeze budget. Under the "Modernization and Renewal Program," the budget would allegedly keep abreast of inflation by rising at a rate of 7 percent a year for five years, starting from a base of $2,143 million in 1973-74. Richardson predicted that the formula, coupled with in-house economies and base consolidations (closing smaller bases and moving their functions to larger ones), would increase the capital portion of the budget to about 18 percent by the end of the five-year period. This was not to happen.

By mid-1974, double-digit inflation had wiped out the small budget increase and left the forces in a worse financial mess than before, particularly in light of increased operational commitments. The problem was compounded in October, when the government ordered a $100 million across-the-board cut in defence spending as part of its war on inflation. Again, defence took the brunt of the assault, while other departments were given substantial increases. A new funding formula had to be found if the forces were ever to improve their buying power. A year later, Richardson claimed he had found it.

On November 27, 1975, Richardson announced that, starting in the next fiscal year, the capital budget would be compensated for inflation and increased, in *real* terms, by 12 percent a year for five years—using a 1976-77 base of $470 million. In the meantime, the capital portion of the budget was running at 11 percent, hardly enough to keep the forces in gas or bullets.

John Gellner, editor of the *Canadian Defence Quarterly,* has told the Commons Defence Committee that in order to keep the forces up to date, $1 should be spent on new equipment for every $2 or $3 allocated to running expenses. He has also noted that the Federal Republic of Germany was considering a policy to "ensure that the investment (capital) portion of the defence budget not fall under 30 percent." France spends about 40 percent of its defence budget on capital costs. Most NATO countries spend between 25 and 30 percent. For the past several years Canada has spent about $1 for every $10, the lowest ratio of any NATO member with forces committed to the Alliance. Ironically, Trudeau's generosity toward the forces helped to create the situation.

Large pay increases for the forces and inflation combined to reduce significantly the amount of money available for new hardware. By the time the troops got paid, there was no more money left in the kitty. In October 1972, amid loud grumblings from bases and stations across the country, the government gave the forces pay parity with the federal public service and linked similar military and civilian jobs to a common wage scale. Servicemen received an 11.5 percent pay boost in two stages to bring them into line.

The raise was an attempt to curb the steady outflow of disenchanted professionals and skilled tradesmen, but the scheme had a drawback. It meant that in order to pay a specialist the going public service wage, it was often necessary to promote him, regardless of the need for another major or sergeant in the command structure.

When the public service won large pay increases in the mid-1970s, military pay kept pace. The result was a comic opera situation which left the traditional pyramid-shaped rank structure bulging at the top as more and more people in a smaller force were promoted to keep abreast of their public service counterparts.

In June 1976, for example, the force had 106 generals—one for every 170 privates. The privates were outnumbered by corporals two to one; there were 1,200 colonels (light and full); senior non-commissioned officers (NCOs) and privates were about even; and there was one officer for every four and a half men, the highest such ratio in the western world. The Canadian serviceman was also the best paid.

Between 1969 and 1976 the average minimum military wage doubled. Personnel costs rose to a staggering 66 percent of the budget, a figure almost double that of other western nations. An untrained private's salary jumped from $2,880 a year to $7,500, an increase of 160 percent. NCO's wages rose more than 110 percent to average about $15,000. Officers' increases were slightly less, about 90 percent, but the average minimum salary for middle-echelon officers (majors) was close to $25,000, with the army of generals earning well up into the $60,000 range.

By the end of 1976, the combined drain on the budget from wages and maintenance costs was 89 percent and the government admitted this was "far too high in any modern armed force. The U.S. is very concerned that their costs in this area are about 46 percent because they regard 48 percent as about the maximum for personnel."[13] In short, there was no money left over to buy badly needed equipment.

British writer Patrick Esmonde-White commented on this bizarre situation in the September 1976 issue of *The Canadian Review.* "The Canadian military," he wrote, "is vastly overstaffed with officers, and they are highly overpaid. This situation has developed over a number of years, and is clearly out of control...If it were true that an army marches on its stomach, then the Canadians should be able to march forever."[14] Obviously, another funding formula was needed.

In January 1977, the government launched an ambitious fifteen year plan, the Defence Services Program, to re-equip the forces with more than 400 badly-needed items—everything from ships and planes to bullets. The budget would remain indexed to inflation and the capital portion would be increased by 12 percent a year *after* inflation until it constituted 20 percent of total defence spending, optimistically by 1981. "It is widely accepted," the government agreed, "that a modern military force must spend a minimum of 20 percent of its budget on new capital equipment if it is to keep pace with technological change."[15]

In explaining details of the plan, Vice-Admiral Robert Falls, then Chief of Defence Staff (CDS) designate, admitted that the forces' purchasing power was still low because of *"the fact the armed forces have been seriously under-funded for the last several years."* As a result, he added, "many purchases that should be made now, have to be deferred. Some of these are urgent, and we must face the fact that some of the equipment in our current inventory will not be replaced until well past the time when it has become uneconomical to maintain it."[16] Credit for the new budget must go to Richardson, who, before he quit the Cabinet because of a row with Trudeau over entrenching French language rights in a revised constitution, fought to get it approved.

After the eleventh hour announcement to buy new equipment, defence critics and the military brass breathed a collective sigh of relief. But in the Fall, when the government started slashing ministerial budgets to convince Canadians it was serious about reducing spending, they began to worry again. Defence Minister Barney Danson quickly soothed them by telling the press, in December, he was confident defence would not be hit. "I think we're all right. I think there's an awareness in Cabinet that we had cut back too far and now we have to make it up."[17] He was wrong.

In April 1978, Conservative defence critic Allan McKinnon revealed that Danson has "double-crossed the armed forces and double-crossed me" by secretly reducing promised spending on new armaments. The MP from Victoria said Danson has maintained he is keeping a long-standing policy promise of increasing real capital spending on defence by 12 percent annually. "However," he said, "when I checked recently with the financial department, I was told the real increase this year is only 2.8 percent. I didn't mind him taking bows for decisions that had been made by former defence minister Richardson as long as the badly-needed new armaments were being acquired."[18]
Later, Danson explained that he had a handshake agreement

*Unless indicated all italics have been inserted by the author.

with Treasury Board President Robert Andras to get an extra $60 million sometime in the future by taking a cut this year. The cut means long-overdue equipment scheduled for purchase in 1978 again has to be delayed. This delay, coupled with inflation and the decline of the dollar, also means Canadians will be paying more for less equipment in the years ahead. McKinnon estimates that delays in the current equipment acquisition program have already added more than $170 million to the cost of new tanks, patrol aircraft and armoured cars.[19]

Federal spending figures indicate that defence was Trudeau's lowest priority. While government spending rose from $10 billion to $45 billion between 1969 and 1978, defence's share crept from $1.8 billion to $3.8 billion, the smallest increase of any department. And while the federal bureaucracy was growing at a record clip, defence manpower was chopped back by a quarter.

Personnel policies also have reflected the low priority Trudeau has assigned to defence. In October 1972, the government reorganized the administrative structure of National Defence Headquarters (NDHQ) in Ottawa, placing civil servants in many top jobs traditionally held by military officers. The reorganization was the result of a year-long study which recommended that parallel civilian and military functions at DND should be integrated to clarify lines of authority and to save money. In reality, it was an attempt to increase civilian control over all aspects of the defence establishment. To the generals it was just another indication that Trudeau did not trust the military to run its own show.

The reorganization created a single command structure at NDHQ, along with a half dozen assistant deputy ministers (ADMs), or "civilian generals." It also elevated a single deputy minister to a position in the military hierarchy equal with the

Chief of the Defence Staff. In the future, the head of many DND departments, including the strictly military, could be either a general or an ADM.

Many high ranking officers resent the creeping "civilianization" of top military posts as unnecessary and an unwelcome incursion into their realm which tends to degrade the increasingly complex "profession of arms" in Canada. They fear their service is slowly being transformed into an adjunct of the public service, with a battalion of ADMs — many without a service background or training — framing military policy, instead of trained officers who better understand the forces.

In 1974, senior colonels J. E. Neelin and L. M. Pederson explained the need to keep a clear distinction between defence policy, made by the government, and military policy which is the internal direction of the forces *by its officers* to execute defence policy:

> Civilians, and specifically civil servants, should have only advisory roles in determining the policies for military training and education, for the selection, distribution and use of military equipment, for the administration of the armed forces, and for strategy and tactics.
>
> To give civilians positions of authority in the military hierarchy is to create civilian generals, a contradiction in terms and a combination of incompatible concepts — it would be as well to have laymen in the College of Physicians and Surgeons.[20]

In the original reorganization the civilian generals were confined mostly to areas of policy and logistics. But by late 1974, following further centralization of administrative powers in the hands of the ADMs, it extended down to the privates in the field. Upset at this trend, the colonels wrote:

> It is (now) therefore the DM and the ADMs who perform the important military functions vis-a-vis the CDS and the commanders.

Their enormous authority reaches down through separate channels to the lowest field units, and there seems to be no way they can be held to account for anything short of calamitous failure. This is because the measure of their effectiveness is the performance of field units, which is the sum of the inextricably interwoven team of combat units and supporting staffs.[21]

Aside from short-circuiting the command structure, the colonels were concerned that the general reorientation of the forces toward national development activities would erode the intrinsic military values that were essential to keep a peace-time force trained and prepared for its principal mission — war:

> Whether the enfeeblement of the armed forces is a matter of concern or not . . . so long as the military are engaged in planning and preparing for the defence of the nation, the need for leadership, loyalty, military administration and especially discipline, is clear and easily understood.
>
> But if their duties are principally to work within the country, building roads, containing floods, conducting youth camps, assisting various welfare schemes, and maintaining law and order, they become similar in outlook and function not just to other government departments but to *all* government departments.
>
> As a consequence, the need for military discipline is no longer obvious, management and business administration supersede leadership and military administration. Worst of all . . . there develops something that is more an armed civil service than an armed force as we have always known them.[22]

Civilianization has not been confined to the top echelon; it now extends to all parts of DND. While the number of regular troops has declined to 78,000 since 1969, the number of full and part-time civilian employees has increased to 37,000 from 35,000. Over the past several years, at bases and stations across the country, civilians have replaced servicemen who were pulled out from base support positions into field units to beef-up the forces' declining "sharp end." It is not a healthy situation because it robs the field units of vital back-up reinforcements if they are ever required.

Civilianization has already damaged the forces' ability to perform their military duties. Just how it will affect them in a time of emergency is anybody's guess, but the generals are clearly worried. In 1974, Brigadier-General D. G. Loomis, then the forces' senior policy analyst, told a closed meeting of the White House Fellows in Washington, D.C.:

> While I have suggested that unification *per se* has not adversely affected our military operational capability, other factors such as force reductions and consequent reorganizations, increased emphasis on civilian management systems as opposed to military command and control and changes in our military roles, activities and tasks have had an impact upon our forces.[23]

And while the forces were slowly being bled to death, another policy was quietly tearing them apart — bilingualism.

Trudeau's bilingualism policies for the forces have had a particularly damaging effect on their over-all efficiency and morale. The policy which originally intended to unite the two language groups in pursuit of a common goal is pushing them farther apart. If the present program continues apace, the forces will be neatly divided into two language camps by the mid-1980s. It has been an expensive and vexatious exercise for most of those in uniform, particularly the English-speaking majority, who believe their careers are being sacrificed on the altar of linguistic expediency.

The program began quietly in the Spring of 1968 when the long-awaited first reports of the Royal Commission on Bilingualism and Biculturalism (B&B) were being discussed. They urged a greater use of French in the everyday affairs of government and the reform-minded Trudeau Liberals were anxious to begin. The armed forces became their target. The forces would be remolded into a completely bilingual organization to become a model for other government departments to emulate. If, in the process, some efficiency and morale had to be sacrificed, this could be corrected later.

On April 2, 1968, Defence Minister Leo Cadieux announced a long-range program to improve the bilingual nature of the forces. The main problem he identified was the fact that French-Canadians (francophones) comprised only 15 percent of the forces, yet more than 27 percent of all recruits were drawn from French Canada. He attributed the francophones' high dropout rate to their general lack of proficiency with English, a requirement for advanced training and promotion, and the "working" language of the forces. Francophones also faced cultural and language problems when posted outside Quebec, so many good soldiers left the forces to avoid moving away.

To overcome these problems the government decided to create a series of French Language Units (FLUs) within the forces, in which a francophone could work and prosper in his mother tongue. Until then, the only unit which worked solely in French was the famous Royal 22nd Regiment (Van Doos), with two battalions at CFB Valcartier, Quebec, and a third in Germany with Canada's NATO brigade. There was a line-up to join the Van Doos and the government felt that other FLUs would encourage more francophones to make a career of the forces if they could do it in their native language.

Cadieux launched the program by announcing that in the summer a Halifax-based destroyer (HMCS Ottawa) would become the forces' first floating FLU, followed by a battalion of the Canadian Airborne Regiment and a squadron of CF-5 fighter aircraft based at Valcartier. Plans were made to establish a French language trades training school at CFB St. Jean, Quebec, later dubbed "Francotrain," to produce French-speaking and bilingual technicians. Cadieux stressed that the bilingual program would be pursued "in such a way that military efficiency and career progression will not be prejudiced and with due regard for the rights and privileges of individuals."[24]

In September 1969 when Cadieux confirmed the new defence priorities, he also revealed the first casualties of the bilingual program. Five English-speaking regiments — among them three of the most famous fighting units in Canadian history — were to be disbanded to make way for the new francophone units. The news sent shockwaves through the Army. With one stroke it would lose the Royal Highland Regiment (Black Watch), Queen's Own Rifles of Canada and the Fort Garry Horse, along with the less celebrated Canadian Guards and 4th Regiment of the Royal Canadian Horse Artillery.

In December 1969 the new Defence Council approved a 10-year plan to speed the spread of bilingualism. The aim was "to ensure that the Canadian Armed Forces reflect the linguistic and cultural values as well as the proportionate representation of both language groups," said the new CDS, General Frederick Sharp, who hoped it would "create a climate wherein military personnel from both language groups will work together toward common goals." To bring the two solitudes closer, the plan called for the eventual establishment of FLUs in all areas of the country but cautioned that bilingualism must "be introduced gradually over a period of years in a manner which will not lead to injustice or misunderstanding." To be avoided at all costs, Sharp warned, was the splitting of the forces into "two unilingual groups confined to geographical areas of the country."[25]

On June 23, 1970, Cabinet adopted recommendations of the B&B Commission's third volume which were to change the character of the forces. The National Defence Act would be amended to reflect the "equality" of the two languages within the forces. English would no longer be the official language of DND. The Royal Commission's report called for the immediate creation of a French language section within Mobile Command (the Army) in which French would be the working language. Other units of the forces were to be designated FLUs and located principally in French-speaking areas, but a few were to be established in other Commands, including NDHQ. Generally, the provision was made for the expansion of French within its own cultural milieu and beyond and a rule established that communications from senior military formations must be sent in the working language of the unit or base receiving them.

These recommendations were implemented within eighteen months. Among them was one that would soon prove controversial. It was recommendation thirty-six which authorized tampering with the merit system for promotion to quickly increase the number of francophones at higher rank levels. Recommendation thirty-six specified:

> a) That (where necessary) to staff the different positions in the French language sector of Mobile Command, qualified personnel who can exercise their duties in French be rapidly promoted; and b) that the authorized rank and promotion quota be adjusted so as to make this possible.[26]

Throughout 1970 the bilingualism program gathered steam. Recruitment was choked off in English Canada and stepped up in Quebec. By 1971 more than a dozen FLUs had been created and plans were made to open many more. But the program was not proceeding fast enough to satisfy Cabinet and in February 1971, General Sharp issued a new "implementation plan to increase bilingualism."[27] It had been drafted by Sylvain Cloutier, DND's civilian deputy minister.

"Equal opportunity," the plan stated, "will be achieved by designating 28 percent of the existing rank structure at all levels and in all areas of responsibilities for francophone personnel."[28] By April 1, 1976, "40 percent of officers of the rank of LieutenantColonel and above, and 35 percent of the remainder of the forces are to obtain the acceptable level four of bilingualism, and 60 and 55 percent respectively by 1980." As a first step a long-range language testing program was launched to determine the bilingual proficiency of all serving members of the forces. Target date for completion was December 1972, when personnel would be classified and an inventory of language resources compiled. The forces would then expand French language training to produce the prescribed percentages of bilingual personnel required under the new implementation plan. In short, to fill quotas.

At the same time National Defence Headquarters began the painstaking process of examining the 34,000 civilian positions in DND to classify those which would require a bilingual employee. Eventually, more than 30 percent were designated bilingual, with a considerably high percentage at NDHQ. But not all were chosen on the basis of need. In 1973 a secretary at the new headquarters building in Ottawa explained how many key positions there became bilingual. After a middle management committee had passed its recommendations to the general in charge of the project, "He said, 'that's not enough,' and with a stroke of his pen he made all directors in defence and their secretaries bilingual positions. Then he went further. He made all positions of directors-general and their secretaries bilingual positions."[29] By September 1, 1972, more than 5,500 servicemen were either taking language training, or were committed to taking it during the 1972/73 academic year.[30]

But in 1972 the program hit an old snag. Despite the

opportunity for rapid promotion, francophones were still leaving the forces at about the same rate as before. Planners were discouraged and in April a new, less ambitious fifteen-year plan was unveiled, complete with revised targets. By the end of the first five years, only 40 percent of generals were to be bilingual, 30 percent of other officers, 20 percent of senior NCOs and 15 percent of privates. By April 1987, the projected percentages for the four categories would be 60, 50, 40 and 25. To achieve this goal, recruitment would be split 50-50 for officers and raised to 40 from 35 percent for francophones from "other" ranks, a discriminatory practice weighted heavily in favour of French-Canadians. However, while planners at NDHQ were busily adjusting targets, unpleasant reports were filtering back from the hinterlands that anglophone troops were getting restless.

Because there was still an annual shortfall in the number of francophone officers and NCOs in the FLUs, the practice of promoting unqualified francophones to fill positions was increasing. Many qualified anglophone troops passed over for promotion were becoming bitter. They were worried about the adverse impact the program was having on their careers and wanted to know when the spate of special accelerated promotions for francophones would stop. The planners were becoming nervous; something had to be done.

In February 1973 teams of officers from NDHQ started a ten-month trek in Halifax that led them to twenty-six bases and stations in Canada and Europe. Their mission was to familiarize personnel with the bilingualism program and sound out problems. The tour was organized by the forces' Director General of Bilingualism and Biculturalism (DGBB), Armand Letellier, who wanted to convince both language groups that the program was being conducted as fairly as possible. More than 7,000 servicemen attended the briefings.

In December 1973, Colonel James Hanna, deputy DGBB, prepared a report on the findings of the grand tour but it was hushed up. The report confirmed that anglophcne personnel were becoming increasingly bitter over accelerated promotions for francophones and morale was becoming a serious problem. The promotion issue had sparked fist-fights between English and French-speaking servicemen and the commanders of several units in English-speaking areas had not made attendance at the briefings compulsory as ordered because the "morale of personnel is already too low to risk generating further discontent."

The "Hanna" report named "deviations from the merit list" which resulted in accelerated promotions for francophones as the "most delicate topic" encountered on tour. "Some personnel . . . with a number of years service say it is the last straw," the report added. Unit commanders were showing increasing resistance to the program because it was interfering with their units' efficiency—they could not spare their best men to go on language courses, reducing their promotion chances and thus creating additional morale problems.

"Some people, and this was frequently heard at more senior levels," the report said, "felt that the goal (promotion targets) was too rigid and was being pursued too slavishly over too short a time frame to the detriment of the forces." French-speaking servicemen also had some doubts about the program.

Francophone officers were beginning to be concerned about the credibility of their promotions in the eyes of their English-speaking peers. Young francophone NCOs were experiencing difficulty exercising their new-found authority over older and often better qualified anglophone subordinates. Everywhere tensions between the two language groups were becoming strained and something had to be done to soothe the situation.

The preliminary report recommended that the B&B program's pace be slackened, but Letellier refused: "I am not recommending any fundamental change of policy as a result of this,"[31] he said. And less than a month later NDHQ informed unit commanders by message that francophone personnel would continue to be given preferential treatment for promotion until government targets were reached. This treatment was to be in accordance with policy spelled out in a confidential memo from the personnel directorate in the fall of 1972: "If it is necessary to deviate from the strict order of merit to achieve an increase in francophone representation, a non-francophone must be bypassed."[32]

By October 1, 1977, the forces had made great strides toward the goal of having 28 percent of their ranks populated by francophones. Since 1970 the proportion of officers had increased from 10.6 percent to 19.2 percent, and men from 19.1 to 24.9 percent.[33] But the cost in money, morale and efficiency has been high.

The program drained millions of dollars from an inflation-battered budget at a time when operational commanders could not afford to buy fuel for their ships and planes. A source close to the last three defence ministers said the program had cost the forces close to $500 million since 1968, including salaries of personnel lost to active duty while on language courses. In 1975, for example, with operational commanders critically short of men, more than 5,000 regular troops were involved in language programs.

In 1972, retired Major General C. Vokes warned of the consequences of pushing bilingualism too far:

> Bilingualism cannot by any stretch of the imagination be classified as a military art, and lack of it a handicap to promotion.
>
> I know of nothing more calculated to destroy morale than to have chances of promotion stifled by inability to speak another language.

If we are to stifle military merit on the altar of bilingualism the present high quality of our armed forces will surely deteriorate.[34]

In 1976, Eugene Deveaux, a Halifax city councillor and former military officer, wrote of the problems which the B&B program had created in the forces:

> I can vouch for the fact that the bilingual program had caused a lot of bad feelings. Some members of the forces have been promoted because of their bilingual qualifications, and these being mainly francophones as opposed to anglophones. This has resulted in many cases in the lowering of morale, particularly with regards to personnel who had worked hard to be promoted, only to find they were bypassed because of their inability to become bilingual.
>
> I have always been under the impression, and I'm sure the public will agree, that our armed forces were and always should be trained and promoted in preparation for war, according to their capabilities, and not according to their ability to speak the French language.[35]

In late 1977, DND accepted recommendations from the Commissioner of Official Languages for speeding up bilingualism in the forces.[36] The government's target year for achieving a 28 percent francophone rank structure is 1987, but the percentage is misleading. Although francophones would make up 28 percent of the total forces, a disproportionate number of them would hold higher positions in the military hierarchy. These positions are literally being saved for them by the quota system.

If targets are reached on schedule, here's how the forces of 1987 would look: 60 percent of all generals would be bilingual; half of all officers would be bilingual, as would 40 percent of NCOs and 25 percent of privates. The CDS would be francophone every other time, according to a former ministerial aide.[37] And in normal practice "bilingual" usually means francophone, as many anglophone servicemen have found out to their chagrin.

Successful completion of language training does not always earn a man the coveted "bilingual" classification on his service records, an important factor for promotion. The present targets are weighted heavily in favour of francophones and appear to block the upward mobility of many deserving anglophones. As Danson confirmed in 1977: "Nobody in the service gets promoted who isn't qualified but everything else being equal, yes, some francophones get the nod in categories where they're under-represented."[38]

Finally, an incident that reveals just how far the authorities are prepared to go in promoting French in the forces occurred last year, when selections for the Order of Military Merit (OMM) were made. The order was created by Trudeau in 1972, when he dispensed with the old British orders "to honour professional excellence and exceptional devotion to duty on the part of members of the Canadian Armed Forces." A committee of senior officers at NDHQ selects the winners after months of discussion and sends the list of names to Government House for routine approval. But in the Spring of 1977 the list came back scrawled with a notation saying, in effect, "Not enough francophones, find more."

"The practice was started a few years ago by the Governor General (Jules Leger)," said an officer involved with the selection. "He won't sign the list unless there are enough French names on it"* After the list came back, an officer placed several discreet phone calls to base commanders in Quebec to find more francophones to decorate. For the past few years the selection

---

*Quoted material that does not have a note number comes from interviews the author carried out with the persons involved. A list of the names of those interviewed is contained at the end of this book.

committee has automatically added francophones to the OMM list when the unofficial quota fell short. "Obviously the last one we sent over didn't have enough," said the officer.

Today, after a decade of neglect, the forces are struggling to perform ever-increasing tasks with diminishing resources. Many top-level officers believe the recently announced meagre increases in manpower and promises of new equipment are inadequate stop-gap measures, designed more to camouflage the true emaciated condition of the forces than to effect a long-range cure.

With manpower and equipment at their lowest levels since the Korean War, can the forces be restored to adequate strength in time to contribute a fair share to collective defence? Perhaps, but the cost of repairing the damage done during the Trudeau decade will take years and cost untold billions. And perhaps that is the real reason why the government appears reluctant to begin, preferring instead to contribute just enough men and material to prevent the forces from collapsing in their tracks.

Just how well—or poorly—the forces have coped with the challenges of the Trudeau years is examined in the following chapters. How well they will perform in the future is unclear. But if the government's track record on defence is any indication, Canada's armed forces could continue to be in retreat for a long time.

# 2 MARITIME COMMAND

The Canadian Navy, known officially as Maritime Command (MARCOM) since unification, is steering a rocky course through troubled waters because of Trudeau's short-sighted maritime defence policies. The decaying fleet is exhausted and past redemption and recent talk about reviving it is as much wishful thinking as political rhetoric. Even if present shipbuilding plans were carried through, the Navy of the next decade would be totally inadequate to handle the anticipated challenges to Canada's vast maritime estates in the near future.

Since coming to power Trudeau has heaped increasing responsibilities on the Navy while cutting its resources in half. He has taken no positive steps to protect Canada's claims to offshore riches aside from bold declarations of ownership, which are meaningless without the power to back them up. Should other nations attempt to ignore Canada's claims and harvest the bounty off our coasts, the present fleet would be hard pressed to stop them—or even keep them under regular surveillance. This situation is ironic because in 1969 it was Trudeau who made protection of national sovereignty the forces'—and particularly the Navy's—principal mission, downgrading its traditional first commitment to NATO and collective defence.

Before 1969 the Navy's ships and patrol aircraft were primarily responsible for surveillance and control of the East and West coastlines, and under the NATO pact, for the North Atlantic sea approaches to North America. The fleet was expert in Anti-Submarine Warfare (ASW), a role it had learned in the Second World War and perfected in the Cold War but which was declared of lesser importance by Ottawa in the new age of détente. It was believed that the Russians no longer posed a serious threat to Canadian sovereignty, so the fleet was ordered to spend more time on domestic duties and less time monitoring the movements of Soviet ships and submarines.

The Navy's new priorities included control of the Arctic and surrounding seas, which added a third coast to its area of responsibility. Recent discoveries of oil and gas in the North had revived Canada's dormant dreams of tapping the riches of its frozen treasure box north of 60 and the Navy was assigned to establish "ownership" of the Far North as oil-hungry Americans were calling Ottawa's claims to the whole area into dispute. The Navy's re-ordered priorities were:

to maintain Canada's sovereignty by surveillance of coastal waters and adjoining ocean areas, including the Arctic archipelago;

to contribute to collective alliance in defence of North America (CANUS) and the North Atlantic (NATO);

to contribute forces to international peace-keeping operations;

to provide emergency communications, quick-reacting transportation, manpower and technical or scientific knowledge in the event of national emergencies or disasters;

to command and train the Naval Reserves stationed in eighteen units from coast to coast;

to command and control the Canadian Rangers.[1]

The new importance of the Navy as a guardian of sovereignty was confirmed in the 1971 White Paper, which also revealed that "the present degree of emphasis on ASW directed against submarine-launched ballistic missiles will be reduced in favour of other maritime roles." In future, the Navy would be re-oriented to provide "a more versatile general purpose capability."[2]

Over the years the Navy's duties were to increase. The three mile offshore limit was pushed to twelve miles. In 1974 Canada joined the International Commission for the Northwest Fisheries (ICNAF) to control over-fishing, and the Navy was ordered to assign warships to police the fishing grounds. To handle the job, MARCOM's commander, Vice-Admiral Douglas S. Boyle, was forced to appropriate a number of destroyers from his tiny West Coast fleet. And in 1977, when Canada extended its offshore fisheries limit and economic zone to 200 miles, the job of policing it fell to the Navy.

But resources did not keep pace with the new demands. In fact, they declined steadily as Trudeau took monies earmarked for ship replacement and renewal to finance other government priorities. Today the fleet is a pale shadow of its former self and faces the bleak prospect of policing the world's longest coastline—18,000 miles—with a handful of overworked men and about twenty operational warships. "Just for the record," Admiral Boyle pointed out in 1977, "we are responsible for 5.8 million square miles . . . or 1/33rd of the earth's surface."[3]

THE THREAT
Canada needs a Navy for many reasons. As a maritime nation sharing the North American continent with the United States, Canada has many responsibilities to protect mariners, its own as well as others; it needs the Navy for this and as an instrument to

enforce compliance with Canadian laws inside the 200-mile limit. A Navy is Canada's ocean-going symbol of national sovereignty, a policeman on the offshore beat establishing ownership, who, if required, is prepared to enforce the rules. Without a Navy Canada could not realistically protect its own coasts or lay serious claims to rich offshore seabeds. Under international law to have is to hold and precedence means a great deal. The U.S. and others already question our claim to all Arctic waters. No matter how confident Ottawa may be with the Canadian case, without our regular "presence" in disputed areas to clearly establish ownership, our legal position gets weaker.

Canada also needs a strong Navy to protect itself from aggression. As a member of NATO dedicated to the defence of the West—including the U.S. nuclear deterrent—the Navy is required to keep a sharp eye on Soviet ships and submarines lurking close to our shores, the price for a place under the U.S. nuclear umbrella. And despite the average Canadian's apparent belief that the Soviets pose no threat to our sovereignty, these feelings are not shared by those who live in the shadow of the Russian bear. Trudeau's sudden shift of priorities away from anti-submarine defence thus came as a shock to defence planners at home and to allies in Europe.

In the late 1960s the Soviet Navy began blossoming from a coastal defence force into a major "blue water" fleet, equipped with a vast array of nuclear-powered warships and submarines. When NATO urged its members to keep their naval defences strong to ensure control of the North Atlantic sea lanes, the government announced it was diverting the Navy to more important domestic duties. Canada's intention to reduce her Navy's ASW capability "was peculiar," noted the prestigious International Institute for Strategic Studies (London), "at a time when the missile-firing submarine is clearly a major threat."[4]

In less than twenty years the Soviet fleet has attained parity with NATO navies and the scales are tipping in their favour. Particularly menacing is the growing fleet of huge nuclear-powered attack submarines, gargantuan hunter-killers armed with wire-guided torpedoes and an array of underwater-launched cruise missiles with enormous range. The Soviet Union has a hundred such subs, each of them to the Nazi U-boat what the computer is to the abacus. In the event of a limited ground war in Europe, NATO troops would immediately need millions of tons of military reinforcements from the U.S. Ninety percent of these would come by sea. To ensure they arrived in time, NATO would need to control the Atlantic sea lanes. Failure to keep them open, a NATO report warns, means "that Russia and the Iron Curtain satellites need only hold down western Europe's defenders for some thirty days. With the powerful Soviet warships blocking the resupply of fuel, food and ammunition, NATO forces in Europe will wither away."[5]

In any kind of East-West conflict, nuclear or conventional, the presence of modern Soviet seapower is disturbing to the West because Russia's wartime aims are easier to achieve than America's. Professor Brian Ranft, a University of London expert in naval affairs, explains: "The Soviet Union does not have to use the sea for strategic purposes; the U.S. does. What the Russians are doing now is creating the capability to deny the use of the sea to the West."[6] Sir Peter Hill-Norton, admiral of the British fleet, adds: "The U.S. has never previously faced a global threat to its sea-lane communications from a mix of subsurface, surface and maritime-air naval forces. This is a strategic change of a kind, not of degree."[7] Former Defence Minister Richardson agreed. In his November 1975 memorandum to cabinet on defence requirements, he said: "The principal maritime threat extending to the shores of North America is that posed by the torpedoes and surface-to-surface missiles carried by the large and highly effective Soviet Attack submarine fleet."* And in 1977, a worried Admiral Boyle said: "On any day there's always two Yankee class (Soviet) submarines within missile range of Chicago," not to mention Canadian cities.[8]

As protection of America's nuclear deterrent is a primary aim of Canadian defence policy, it seemed logical to assume the government would equip its Navy to guard against the principal threat to that deterrent—nuclear submarines. But it did not. Today, after years of urging by its own naval experts and Washington, the government still has not moved to plug under-ice channels in the Arctic through which Soviet submarines can move undetected into prime target range of American cities. In 1970 Cabinet rejected as too costly a recommendation by the Commons' subcommittee on Maritime Forces, which said the Navy required a capability to "ensure prompt detection of all surface, subsurface and seabottom activity," particularly in the North. It would have been relatively inexpensive to develop and install underwater sonar instruments at key channels to catch a Soviet nuclear submarine churning along beneath the ice. The government believed there was no threat, but subsequent facts prove them wrong.

Since the early seventies Admiral Boyle and his predecessor, Rear-Admiral Robert Timbrell, warned Cabinet that the presence of huge Soviet fishing fleets off Canada's coasts presented a real danger to national security. They wanted the fleets' movements restricted from sensitive inshore waters, but Cabinet refused on the grounds that such action could damage Canada-Soviet relations. The admirals knew the Soviets were

---

*On November 9, 1975, Richardson sent a detailed "Memorandum to the Cabinet" on "The Defence Program — Force Structure," which reviewed the Government's defence policies and spelled out options for the future develop-ment of the Forces. From here on it is referred to as Richardson's memo.

constantly over-fishing in Canadian waters, yet lacked the manpower to keep a watchful eye on their movements. For years Soviet fishermen cruised undetected into fishing areas reserved for Canadians, reaping in a few hours enormous quantities of fish, then disappearing into the twilight. Whenever caught in the act or off course, their excuse was always the same: navigator's error. This answer puzzled the admirals, who could not understand how such sophisticated vessels bristling with antennae could get lost so often. Just what were they up to?

In 1972, a report by Canadian writer Commander W.G. Kinsman in the respected *U.S. Naval Institute Proceedings,* explained that the fleets provided a screen for "spy ships whose sole role is to gather electronic intelligence." They also contain a healthy sprinkling of "oceanographic survey ships, ostensibly charting fishing grounds and studying the environmental conditions for pure research. These ships are welcomed into our ports in the name of the brotherhood of science, but it is not beyond the realm of possibility that their primary role is to study the potential fighting grounds for their submarines. . . .

"Still another problem posed by these fishermen is their ability to shelter and camouflage the movement of their submarines... into, for example, the Davis Strait and even into Hudson Bay... from that area, the submarine-launched ballistic missile can reach Canada and the industrial centres of the United States."[9]

Suspicions were confirmed in July 1976, when the world learned officially that Soviet fishing fleets were operational components of the Red Navy. In a rare interview with *Pravda,* Admiral Sergei G. Gorshkov, architect and chief of Russia's modern navy, confirmed that "maritime transportation, fishing and scientific research on the sea are part of the Soviet Union's naval might." And in his recent book, *The State's Sea Power,* Gorshkov highlighted the increasing "ability of the Soviet state to make effective use of the world ocean in the defence of socialism against imperialist aggression."[10]

While declaration of the 200-mile limit has made it easier for the Navy to keep track of Soviet vessels, the threat of covert submarine activity in the Arctic has increased dramatically. A NATO report issued in 1977 said it appeared certain that "USSR submarines have found a passage under the Polar ice to enable them to transit from their northern bases into ice-free waters west of Greenland. The passage would take them north of Greenland and Ellesmere Island, south in Kane Basin and Baffin Bay. The advantages of such a route would be two-fold. It would enable submarines moving into North American waters to circumvent the planned defensive operations of the Supreme Allied Commander Atlantic, (SACLANT) in the Greenland-Iceland-United Kingdom Gap . . . such craft could manoeuvre into firing positions where their missiles could be effective over a much larger portion of North America."[11]

Before this, Soviet subs could only reach the open sea through the "Gap," the Dardanelles and the Sea of Japan and there, their trails were picked up by lurking U.S. subs and patrol planes. If the NATO report is true, it means Soviet subs can slip unnoticed into Canada's backyard because there are no subsurface sonar devices set to detect them. It is common knowledge that U.S. nuclear submarines use the waters of the Northwest Passage without informing Ottawa, both as strategic exercises and to underscore U.S. claims to the area. It is also likely that the Soviets do the same thing.[12] The only known counter to such a threat, the NATO report concluded, "would be to deploy nuclear powered attack submarines on the passage route." When Cabinet rejected placing underwater detection devices in the North, it also turned down a secret proposal from the U.S. to buy a half-dozen used hunter-killer nuclear submarines for such a purpose at bargain rates.

What all this means for Canada, Admiral Boyle said in 1977, "is that if we want to protect our sovereignty, we've got to know where they (boats and subs) are, and what they're up to." Underscoring his need for more ships and men, he added: "On any day, there are 300 to 400 ships inside the Canadian area of surveillance on the East coast alone, and 20 to 50 percent of them will be Soviet."[13]

In February 1977, Vice-Admiral Falls told a Calgary audience that Canada must beef up its naval defences or face the prospect of losing its maritime riches to starving nations. Commenting on Russia's known over-fishing off the East Coast and in view of predicted crop failures in the near future, he said: "What would nations with hungry populations do? Would they observe the niceties of the ICNAF Fisheries Agreement of law-of-the-sea regulations and stay within their official quotas and within their own fishing zones? ...Or would they fish where and how it suited them? *Unless of course, the coastal nation concerned had the power to stop them. . . .*

"But the power to use force must exist, and potential transgressors of Canadian sovereignty must be convinced that Canada will use force if all other alternatives are ineffective. A nation cannot have partial sovereignty any more than a woman can be a little bit pregnant. It is all or nothing."[14]

Admiral Timbrell believes the Soviet's maritime "troika" of a modern navy, fishing fleet and merchant marine "can dominate the world . . . economically and militarily," unless Canada and other western nations are willing to spend more to police their own waters.

Completing the triangle of Soviet mastery of the high seas is the burgeoning Russian merchant service, an arm of the Red Navy, which is slowly gaining control of free-world shipping. Western fleets cannot compete with the Russians because their ships are designed and built by the state, manned by their own crews and fueled from cheap domestic sources. As more and more western business goes to the "bargain-priced" Soviet merchantmen, Russia's control of the seas and international trade increases.

Should East-West relations deteriorate, Russia could be in a powerful position to damage western economies — a stated intention of consecutive Soviet leaders. By blocking re-supply lines to Europe, it could blackmail NATO into backing off while it absorbed border states, and force other concessions around the world. If such a scenario sounds bizarre, the authoritative *Janes's Fighting Ships* recently alerted its readers to the age-old lessons of seapower: "Those who have the capacity to interrupt this international intercourse will remain, as always in the past, in a position to achieve their ends. The argument that war is unthinkable in this nuclear age applies less to the sea than to any other area . . . without any overt conflict, without the firing of any guns or missiles or torpedoes, great areas of the oceans can be declared, or exercises conducted which can adversely affect the flow of shipping. Delays will result in increased prices; interference in increased premiums. With 98 percent of the bulk of the world's trade being carried in ships it needs little emphasis to show the disastrous effects of any or all these acts, none of which reaches the definition of war. *To conduct trade with security a country needs the manifest capability to defend its own, whether that be shipping lanes, fishing area, its oil rigs, or the coastal traffic upon which much depends in so many areas.*"[15]

For a trading nation like Canada, which lacks its own merchant marine yet has the world's longest coastline, the need to maintain an adequate Navy appears self-evident, particularly in view of the rise of Soviet seapower. Trudeau's naval advisers — and allies —warned him about the dangers inherent in not maintaining the Navy at acceptable levels. The challenge and the threat were known, but the Navy is still fading away.

## DECLINE OF THE FLEET

The decline of the Navy started in 1969, when the defence budget was frozen for three years. Forced to economize in the face of rising wages, inflation and increased operational demands, the Navy cannibalized itself to stay afloat, consuming stores, spares and ammunition that were not replaced for lack of funds. When the ribs began to show and the pulse grew weak, ships were laid up to give the body a rest, yet the condition became worse. For the first time in a decade men were leaving the Navy faster than they could be replaced. Morale, along with the ailing fleet, began to sink.

Vice-Admiral A. L. Collier, who succeeded Boyle in July 1977, is the busiest commander in the forces. From his cramped headquarters in Halifax, he controls naval and air forces which are responsible for three coasts. Unlike the army and air force, which have limited operational roles in peacetime, the Navy must perform its sovereignty tasks every day, rain or shine, without a break. A look at the admiral's daily operational duties tells the story.

Admiral Collier wears four hats. As chief of MARCOM, with responsibilities for maritime sovereignty, he cooperates with U.S. forces for the defence of North America against seaborne attack. On the West Coast, he exercises his authority through the Commander, Maritime Forces Pacific (MARPAC) at Esquimalt (Victoria), B.C., which includes responsibility for all waters running 200 miles off the coasts from Alaska to the U.S. border.

Second, he wears a NATO hat for his role as Commander of the Canadian Atlantic Sub Area (CANLANT), a subordinate command of SACLANT, which embraces 502,000 square miles of the North Atlantic. In addition, the admiral supplies at least one ship on a continuing basis to the Standing Naval Force Atlantic (STANFORLANT), a squadron of ships from several

NATO nations operating together continuously to develop experience as a multinational force.

Third, he wears the hat of Regional Commander and is responsible for a host of local duties such as aid to civil power, assisting other government departments, pollution control and more. He is also chief of the Naval Reserve's eighteen divisions located in major cities across the country, a job he inherited in 1969.

Finally, the admiral wears a fur hat as commander of the Canadian Rangers, who are scattered up and down the Pacific and Atlantic coasts. The Rangers, located in remote arctic settlements, are controlled by the Commander of the Northern Region, based at Yellowknife, N.W.T. Revived by the government in the early 1970s, the Rangers are optimistically described as "a vital source of intelligence in the wilderness . . . either in war or in the role of protection of sovereignty."[16] They are a small group of natives who are commissioned to report any suspicious objects lurking about the tundra. For their trouble, MARCOM ensures they receive annually 200 rounds of ammunition for their government-supplied surplus .303 rifles.

In a sense the increased emphasis on maritime defence and northern sovereignty recast the Navy in its historic posture as principal guardian of the nation, a role which had passed to triumphant air power during the Second World War. With development of sophisticated missile-carrying ships and far-ranging patrol aircraft, the modern navy has regained some of its former lustre and feels itself once again to be the senior service. In 1969, however, as the fleet gathered steam to meet the challenges of the Seventies, storm clouds were gathering on the horizon.

When Trudeau turned defence priorities northward and coastward, the Navy's strength stood at more than 17,000 officers and men, seventy-one fixed-wing aircraft and a fleet of twenty-eight modern warships, including the 20,000-ton aircraft carrier HMCS Bonaventure, fresh from refitting. It was not a big fleet, but it possessed enough flexibility and depth to perform everything from ASW surveillance off both coasts and control of the twelve-mile limit, to fielding a carrier group to exercise with NATO allies on the high seas.

On the East Coast, based at Halifax, Bonaventure headed the fleet's ASW team, which consisted of nine helicopter-carrying destroyers (DDHs)and four destroyer-escorts (DDEs) in various stages of a modernization program. Most of the 3,000-ton destroyers were equipped with Canadian designed variable-depth sonar for tracking submarines and all were less than fifteen years old. Naval architects and planners consider twenty years to be the operational lifespan of a modern warship; after that it becomes increasingly expensive to maintain as its combat capability declines.

Also based at Halifax were three new "0" class conventionally-powered submarines, purchased from Britain in the mid-1960s to provide operational training for the fleet's ASW forces. The six-year-old, 20,000-ton supply ship HMCS Provider supported the fleet at sea, while the jetty-bound repair ship HMCS Cape Scott provided in-harbour maintenance. The experimental hydrofoil warship HMCS Bras d'Or was a source of wonder and amusement to sailors as it sped around the harbour on its glittering foils at fantastic speeds.

On the West Coast, seven DDEs and an assortment of occasionally activated reserve training ships basked in the Pacific sun, only now and again searching for the vintage submarine HMCS Grilse, on loan from the United States Navy for fleet ASW training.

The Navy also keenly awaited the arrival of several new Canadian-built ships, all ordered in the late 1960s as part of

Hellyer's five-year, $1.5 billion re-equipment program, of which the Navy's share was approximately $460 million.

Aside from two 24,000-ton supply ships, Protecteur and Preserver, which would join the fleet in 1970, excitement centred around four new Tribal class (DDH-280) helicopter-destroyers that would bolster the Atlantic fleet in 1972-73. At 4,200 tons, the gas-turbine powered Tribals were the biggest warships ever designed and built in Canada, and have since proven to be the most trouble-free and effective vessels of their size in the world. Carrying two Sea King helicopters, they could patrol twice the area of a conventional DDH and considerably more than a DDE.

But ships are only part of MARCOM's over-all surveillance capability, representing in a sense the control arm of maritime sovereignty. The other vital component was supplied by six squadrons of patrol aircraft which carried out far-ranging, round-the-clock aerial surveillance off both coasts. Teamed with ships, they were credited with a considerable defence capability against conventional submarines, although detection and tracking of nuclear submarines was proving less successful as time and technology passed them by. Most of the Navy's patrol aircraft belonged to a former generation, their electronic avionics systems rapidly approaching obsolescence.

In 1969 the naval air arm consisted of seventy-one fixed-wing airplanes — thirty-two Argus long-range patrol aircraft (LRPAs), operating from three squadrons on the East Coast and one on the West — and one squadron of thirty-nine Tracker short-range patrol aircraft. The carrier-borne Trackers, along with a squadron of Sea King helicopters, were removed from Bonaventure at the end of 1969 and based ashore. Some of the large and versatile Sea Kings returned to sea duty, flying ASW missions from DDH destroyers and supply ships. The four-engine Argus and twin-engine Tracker both came into service in the late 1950s.

In April 1969, the Navy's resources shaped up like this:

| | Ships | | | | Aircraft | |
|---|---|---|---|---|---|---|
| | East | West | | | East | West |
| Carrier | 1 | | Argus | | 26 | 6 |
| DDHs | 9 | | Tracker | | 39 | |
| DDEs | 4 | 7 | Other* | | | |
| Provider | 1 | | | | | |
| Cape Scott | 1 | | | | | |
| Subs | 3 | 1 | | | | |
| Bras d'Or | 1 | | | | | |
| | 20 | 8 (28) | | | 65 | 6 (71) |

*About forty helicopters in several squadrons operate from ships and shore based in a support role. They are not included as general fixed-wing patrol aircraft. In addition, the Navy's total ship inventory included about 100 auxiliaries, ranging from research vessels on loan to other departments to small passenger ferries, such as the "bird" class boats used for transporting naval and dockyard personnel across harbours.

Riding high at the end of a five-year equipment renewal program, the Navy's future appeared rosy, despite a fixed budget for three years. After all, with the new ships on the horizon and declarations of maritime sovereignty ringing throughout the land, what could go wrong?

### BONAVENTURE FAREWELL

The Navy's first major casualty of 1969 was the carrier Bonaventure, which the government ordered to be sold or scrapped by 1970, less than three years after her controversial $18 million "half-life refit and modernization . . . to make her fully operational into the 1970s."[17]

The Bonnie "was just one of the first casualties of this inflationary trend and the budget freeze," said Paul Hellyer in 1976, the man who had ordered the refit a decade earlier. "You couldn't replace it today for many times that amount of money ($18 million). If it hadn't been for inflation and that they couldn't afford to pay for the men or the fuel to run it . . . it would still be in operation today."

The ship was purchased from Britain in 1952 for $18 million and outfitted as an ASW carrier. She was commissioned in Belfast on January 17, 1957, and arrived in Halifax on June 27 as the first fully Canadian-owned carrier. From the start of her thirteen years with the Atlantic fleet, the Bonnie was an invaluable ASW and general-purpose ship. Her squadrons of Tracker aircraft and Sea King helicopters could mount a considerable aerial surveillance on short notice; she was useful for pilot training, search and rescue and troop transportation. In addition, her high-profile presence off the coast quietly underscored claims to maritime sovereignty. According to Admiral Timbrell, losing Bonaventure reduced "by a quarter" the fleet's over-all ASW capability at a single stroke.

Timbrell also feels Bonaventure's premature demise cost the fleet an important "armed" sealift capacity for peacekeepers and other troops. He was in command of Bonaventure in 1964 when she transported urgently needed Canadian peacekeeping troops to Cyprus at the request of the United Nations. The carrier meant "we had the capability to lift our own men and equipment where and when they are needed — the Bonnie was fully armed — and she could have backed us up in a limited way." He believes the ship was "good for ten or twelve more years."

What Canada lost, said Commodore Frank Caldwell,* "was a

---

*Caldwell, now director of programs for the Navy League of Canada, is editor of the *Maritime Affairs Bulletin* and former Commander of the Fifth Destroyer Squadron. He is an acknowledged expert on maritime defence policies and enjoys close links with NDHQ.

general usage utility ship. She didn't represent any extra expense. The Trackers were there, the ship was there . . . she could be used as a transport, used to fuel or supply ships at sea. You could send her away on an extended mission with three or four destroyers and she could mother them," effectively extending their range many times.

"We've certainly got no means of lifting our troops out of the Middle East if somebody decided they're going to be kicked out or get into trouble," he said. "The Bonnie was a self-contained fighting vehicle; now we're dependent on friendly airfields, and friendly shipping to get our own people out of trouble spots."

An integral part of Hellyer's "global-mobile" force, the Bonnie was refitted at the Davie shipyards in Quebec from April 23, 1966 to April 27, 1967, at a cost of $18 million, or about $10 million more than originally approved by Treasury Board. She was sold in 1970 to a Vancouver scrap dealer Bill Kennedy for $850,000 after the government failed to find a better buyer. Kennedy promptly resold the ship to a Taiwan scrapyard for $1.6 million.

Following criticism that the government had not tried very hard to find a buyer, defence critic John Gellner noted: "I absolutely refuse to accept the official statement that no foreign government can be found which would pay a decent price — or indeed any price — for the ship," pointing out that Argentina had just paid $4 million for The Karl Doorman, a rundown British-built carrier of similar vintage. "This would be tantamount to saying that once Gordon Sinclair has bought his latest Rolls-Royce, no more can be sold in Toronto."[18]

The September 1969 decision to retire Bonaventure as "surplus" to Canadian needs was an expensive exercise in reverse logic. In an effort to keep defence spending to a minimum, the government felt that it was better to use the Bonnie's 1,000 officers and men to crew the four new Tribals that would soon appear, rather than recruit another 1,000 men to man them.[19]

With weaponry and classified equipment removed, the Bonnie was towed from Halifax harbour on October 28, 1970, arriving in Taiwan on March 19, 1971. But nobody knows for sure if she was ever broken up. During the past few years reports have filtered back to Canada that the Bonnie has been spotted in South Asian waters as a fully operational warship. Defence officials deny the rumours, but some Conservative MPs, including Michael Forrestall (Dartmouth-Halifax East) are not convinced. He has reported rumours that the Taiwanese swapped the Bonnie with India for an aging carrier of a similar class. Nobody really knows. The government was unable to send an official to Taiwan to witness the actual breakup because diplomatic relations had broken off over Canada's recognition of Red China.[20]

Regardless of whether Canadians are now shaving with the remains of the Bonnie's hull, or if she's plying foreign waters under a new flag, her untimely passing severely reduced the Atlantic fleet's sealift and ASW capability at a time when it was badly needed.

### SINKING OF BRAS D'OR

Moving from the Navy's biggest ship to its smallest hope, the government next axed the high-flying experimental hydrofoil warship Bras d'Or after successful sea trials and $53 million of research and development. The project was started in 1961 to develop an inexpensive, fast and highly manoeuvrable ship for ocean surveillance and ASW work. On July 9, 1969, after overcoming setbacks and a $6 million fire which destroyed the original prototype, Bras d'Or sped down Halifax harbour and into the open Atlantic at seventy-two miles an hour to become the world's fastest warship.

Two years later, however, the government mothballed the project for five years "because re-assessment of Maritime Command's requirements has scaled down its priority."[21] The ship was beached on a Halifax wharf where the bright red "400" on her sleek grey hull has faded to a washed out pink.

When the project was killed, Canada was a leader in hydrofoil design, and the only NATO country to have a fully operational hydrofoil warship of her type in commission. Once in production, ten ships would have gone to the Navy for patrol and ASW work at an estimated cost of $20 million each, or about one-third the 1974 price of a new destroyer.

Why did Canada cancel a project that had already cost $53 million and had produced promising results? Defence Minister Donald Macdonald said export sales did not look promising because "some foreign countries which had shown an interest in the Canadian project" have made it clear that hydrofoils are "well down on their priority list," and he was reluctant to spend another "$20 million or more" to get ships into production.[22] But this was not the case. Several foreign countries, including the U.S., Germany and Italy, were rushing into hydrofoil development,* a fact Macdonald himself had noted months earlier.

"There is still a high level of NATO interest in this hydrofoil development concept,"[23] he said in July 1971. In March, he told a magazine: "DND has been encouraged by the recent level of foreign interest in this project. It would appear that other nations are becoming increasingly aware of the potential of a

---

*In 1973, the Boeing Co. in the U.S. received a $42.6 million contract from the American Navy to design a missile-carrying hydrofoil for use by NATO countries. It is now building a craft slightly bigger than Bras d'Or. Grumman Aerospace Corp. is also producing a sixty-seven-ton gunboat which may be used by German and Italian navies.

hydrofoil-type craft."[24] And in 1970, an enthusiastic Leo Cadieux had said, "we are going ahead with the hydrofoil program, for despite her teething problems, the Bras d'Or shows considerable promise as a cost-effective ASW weapon."[25] The real reason Cabinet killed Bras d'Or, said Caldwell, is "because they wanted to spend the money on other projects."

Was Bras d'Or really successful? According to the men who designed and sailed the 200-ton ship, she was. Despite initial problems with her foils, Michael Eames, head of the hydronamics section, Defence Research Establishment in Dartmouth, N.S., said Bras d'Or's sea trials were beautiful and validated the basic design concept of the ship. They demonstrated its ability to operate at sea-state-5 (ten foot seas) in the open ocean and with the seakeeping quality of a destroyer-escort.[26]

If the government was worried about the $20 million price tag per ship, Eames explained, certain economies could have been worked into the production program. "Cost goes up very steeply when you consider a vessel capable of more than fifty knots," he said. "If you are prepared to sacrifice, say, ten knots, we can save construction costs of $10 million."[27]

Fifty knots is approximately sixty miles an hour, which is still faster than almost anything afloat. As an engineer aboard the Bras d'Or said in 1970: "It is too early to be certain what the Bras d'Or may lead to, but any ship that can operate in the North Atlantic at speeds up to and over fifty knots cannot be ignored."[28]

From MARCOM's standpoint, the hydrofoil ship would have fitted well into its wider role or reconnaissance, fisheries and environmental protection. It would also have yielded considerable savings in operational crew requirements at a time when the Navy is starved for men. One hydrofoil could operate with thirty to forty men, compared with the more than two hundred needed for a slower destroyer.[29]

Rear-Admiral R.H. Leir, a former commander of MARPAC, still feels the hydrofoil is the answer to keeping Canada's 200-mile limit under surveillance, particularly in light of the increasing proliferation of Soviet ships off both coasts. "Canada's contribution (in the North Atlantic) should primarily be one of intelligence-gathering and surveillance. Just about the only viable surface surveillance vehicle is the hydrofoil. It's ideal for patrolling the fence. It combines the loitering power and the presence of a ship with the manoeuvrability and jump-time of an aircraft."[30] The Americans agree.

The United States Navy "not only have a continuing program for six hydrofoil craft but are also actively developing the equipment for their use in an ASW role," reported the Navy League in December 1977. "In the meantime two ex-USN hydrofoils . . . have been taken over by the U.S. Coast Guard for evaluation trials. Their role in the U.S. Coast Guard would presumably be for patrol of the 200-mile fishery zone — for which tasks they seem eminently suited. Is Canada dropping out of the hydrofoil picture too soon?"[31]

Admiral Leir concludes: "Unfortunately, we lost courage and gave up this very promising research with the Bras d'Or . . . we have lost courage so many times in the past just when pure research was about to blossom into new equipment."[32]

Paul Hellyer agrees. "Killing Bras d'Or when they did was a tragic mistake . . . it's an example of how little in a sense (Canadians) are ready to accept pure research and development when they know about it in large gobs."

The need for a light and fast patrol warship was comically underscored on November 8, 1976, when the 4,200-ton Tribal HMCS Iroquois was dispatched from Halifax to catch a trio of fleeing Cuban fishing boats which had been spied fishing illegally in Canadian waters. "It becomes an expensive exercise in overkill," remarked one respected defence writer in Halifax, "especially when the warship has a daily payroll of about $4,000" and carries a crew of 280 men.[33] The unofficial cost of the farcical chase was close to $20,000.[34]

Whither Bras d'Or? In 1976 Richardson announced it would be kept "in a state of preservation for a further five years until a final decision is made on the future of hydrofoils in the Canadian Forces. The annual cost of that preservation is $30,000."[35]

### THE MEN

By March 1973, the strains of three fixed budgets was starting to show. Throughout the Navy the inventory of warships had reached thirty for the first time in several years with the arrival of four new Tribals and two new supply ships. But the glow soon faded as four seaworthy destroyers (DDEs Chaudiere, Columbia and St. Croix, and DDH St. Laurent) were mothballed to "ready reserve" to provide crews for the new arrivals.

Lack of trained manpower became critical as attrition and the government's "planned reduction program" saw the Navy's strength fall to below 14,000 officers and men, the lowest figure in twenty years. Despite hard-sell recruiting for the glamorous sea trades, the Navy began losing trained men at a rate of 1,000 a year, and the trend seemed irreversible.

"One of the most urgent problems to solve," cried the Navy League, "is that of improving the retention rate of trained personnel. Modern ships with sophisticated equipment require highly skilled operators and maintenance staff . . . if they choose to leave the service in an early phase of their careers it is time-consuming and expensive to train replacements. Some of the senior officers look upon this as the major cause for anxiety in to-day's Maritime Forces."[36]

Admiral Timbrell blamed the initial freeze period and restricted recruiting as the two policies that hurt his command most. "The impact of the freeze started to hit us in 1973," he said. "On paper I had twenty-four destroyers but I could only sail twelve of them because of a manpower shortage and high maintenance requirement."

To keep his ships operational, Timbrell scavenged men from every corner of his command — fleet schools, offices, depots, the reserve — but this stop-gap measure further aggravated the manpower problem. For the first time in years, sailors were spending most of their time at sea. The normal ratio of 60-40 (60 percent at sea, 40 percent at home) reached 70-30 and was still climbing. Some destroyers sailed with fewer than 150 men aboard. To avoid a perpetual life at sea, many men retired early, particularly the vitally needed technicians. And there were other problems.

"The actual maintenance of the ships had to be delayed," said Timbrell, "because funds weren't available to put them through as quickly as required. And stockpiles of spares started to dry up. That's bad because if you hold off buying spares for seven or eight years, it's going to take another seven or eight years to recover. We're so far behind in spares today that it will cost us a fortune . . . and take years to recover."

### THE CRISIS
The initial freeze ended in fiscal year 1972-73. For the Navy it was a period of declining numbers and increasing tasks "with particular emphasis on sovereignty and the environment."[37] Aside from normal coastal patrols, both ships and aircraft struggled to fulfil new roles such as northern surveillance, pollution control and, for the Trackers, counting caribou and geese for the department of environment.[38] How critical was the situation? The Navy League reported:

"The cost of operations was consistently more critical as the funds resources for fuel were stretched beyond limits, and were reflected in forced constraints on flying hours and sea time for aircraft and ships. The Argus carrying out northern patrols do so at the expense of their primary role, that of ocean surveillance, and have been seriously reduced in the flying hours available for anti-submarine training and air-sea cooperation. *Any reductions of operations below the level which was achieved would not only have resulted in a failure to meet our commitments, but would also have resulted in a serious degradation of our basic training and operational expertise."*[39]

The Navy's general capability was already sinking when Admiral Boyle took over from Timbrell in August 1973. Boyle immediately started to shore it up but within three months of his new command he was clobbered by the government's "modernization and renewal program."

On October 10, 1973, Richardson announced the long-awaited details of the first post-freeze defence budget. It would rise by 7 percent a year for five years to compensate for inflation, but surprisingly there was no mention of new ships or increased manpower for a weary fleet. Instead, as its share of the "renewal" program, the Navy would lose its four idled destroyers by the end of 1974, and see its Tracker aircraft fleet stripped of valuable electronic ASW gear and reduced to sixteen from thirty-three early in 1974. In addition, the West Coast training submarine HMCS Rainbow was to be removed from service.[40]

Admiral Boyle was less than pleased with the news. "It doesn't make sense to me," he said, "that we are doing away with half our Tracker force and four of our destroyers when the Canadian government announces that it will go to the Law of the Sea Conference in Caracas (in 1974) to demand a 200-mile limit to our territorial waters."[41]

In 1974 the Navy's anemic condition became worse. Manpower dropped below 13,000 regulars. Double-digit inflation and soaring oil prices crippled the modestly increased defence budget, forcing operational economies. Boyle pleaded for help and received none. When Richardson boasted to a reporter that "it's quality, not quantity that counts . . . the Navy would acquit itself well in the event of armed conflict because its men and equipment are second to none,"[42] Boyle dryly pointed out that his seagoing strength had shrunk to "5,100 men — about 100 more than the crew of the U.S. carrier Independence."[43]

#### FOUR FOR THE ROAD

The most visible economy of this period was the final disposal of four seaworthy destroyers because of the lack of funds and manpower to sail them. To admirals Boyle and Timbrell, it seemed inconceivable that at a time "when NATO countries are so concerned about . . . the expanding Soviet fleet; when the question of safe delivery of oil from the Middle East is everyone's worry and at a time when the Minister of Environment (Jack Davis) seeks to extend Canada's offshore jurisdiction to 200 miles, we are suddenly told that Canada proposes to reduce its fleet by selling four ships. The reason: we are short of men to man them."[44]

Loss of the destroyers downgraded Canada's potential contribution to SACLANT, the nation's main maritime shield in event of war. The government claimed it was dumping the ships in accordance with a long-standing manning plan that called for their replacement with the four new Tribals.[45] Not so, said Timbrell, who as Maritime Commander at the time needed "every ship I could get . . . no such plan existed." Caldwell confirmed that "the original program for the 280s envisaged them as being additional to the twenty destroyers then available. This would upgrade our contribution to SACLANT. In 1964 our commitment to SACLANT was a carrier and thirty-two destroyers . . . today it's in the order of about eight ships."

Despite government assurances that the ships would be kept in ready reserve if a buyer couldn't be found, a memo from NDHQ appears to confirm suspicions that Cabinet intended to junk the ships as soon as possible. The memo, dated October 13, 1973, was signed by General Dextraze. It reads: "In accordance with ministerial direction, the aim is to implement the disposal of the HMCS St. Laurent, Columbia, Chaudiere and St. Croix to help finance the defence program." A year later, however, the government gave in to Opposition pressure and scrapped only the St. Laurent. The other three were banished to the "black squadron" where their innards have played a helpful role in keeping sister ships afloat.

While financial restraints imposed in 1974 bruised the hardworking Atlantic fleet, they knocked out the tiny West Coast navy as far as operational capability went. When Ottawa handed the Navy the job of using East Coast warships on fisheries inspection patrols under the ICNAF pact, Admiral Boyle was forced to denude his tiny Pacific fleet of its DDHs to handle the job. By the end of the year all twelve DDHs had been grouped in Halifax. This left only eight DDEs at Esquimalt, half of which were languishing half-manned in the Training Group, reducing the "yacht squadron's" general surveillance capability by more than one third. That capability was still more reduced months later when the government returned the fleet's lend-lease training submarine Rainbow to the Americans, in order to free her sixty-odd submariners for duty with the three "0" class boats in Halifax. The Rainbow's passing, noted the Navy League, "caused a serious gap in ASW training of ships and aircraft on the West Coast, particularly in view of the impossibility of obtaining target submarine time from heavily committed allied submarine forces."[46] The situation still exists.

With more to do and less to do it with, the Navy was dealt another blow in the Fall of 1974. In an attempt to slow the pace of inflation, the government ordered a $100 million across-the-board cut in defence spending. Despite Admiral Boyle's protest that he was already hard pressed to meet his commitments, his budget was axed by $6.8 million — about 10 percent — and he was told to cope.

The timing of the cut created problems. Because it was applied so late in the fiscal year, noted the Navy League, "it meant a cutback of between 20 and 30 percent in some quarters," which resulted in reduced training and operations.[47] To keep his ships and aircraft operational, although at reduced levels, Admiral Boyle launched an in-house conservation program that included:

removing half the lights from dockyard offices;
typing all letters on both sides of the paper;
unplugging a bank of lights in his own office;
reducing the speed of ships and aircraft to save fuel;
restricting the use of staff cars and trucks to save gas;
cancelling gunnery practice for the fleet; and
opting out of NATO exercises.

The program was only partly successful and contributed to the decline of manpower, as men left the service to avoid spending most of their lives at sea. Forward bases were closed down and Admiral Boyle began scraping what little fat remained on MARCOM's bones. But despite his ruthless economy drive in search of money for fuel, ships and aircraft sat paralysed for months, leaving great chunks of coastline untended for extended periods. These are a few examples of reduced operations:

From October to December 1974, Arctic surveillance flights by Argus LRPAs were completely eliminated to save fuel, but were resumed in January, at the rate of one a month, after protests from Opposition MPs.[48]

At sea, destroyers reduced speed by day and the new Tribals stopped their engines after sunset and drifted into the dawn.

In October, the 2nd Battalion of the Royal Canadian Regiment was left high and dry on a New Brunswick wharf when the Navy suddenly withdrew from a combined exercise. The reason: "The very important operational sealift of the battalion and its equipment to Newfoundland could not be carried out because of cutbacks in naval fuel allocations." So the exercise was switched to "a hastily improvised forest training area in Nova Scotia."[49]

Of this period, the Navy League reported: "MARCOM has insufficient personnel for its tasks, and yet there seems little chance of reducing commitments without further endangering of national security."[50] Aware of this, Admiral Boyle reluctantly cancelled the Navy's annual "spring training exercise in Puerto Rican waters" for the first time in more than a decade, in order to save fuel for domestic patrols.[51] "The Navy would either opt into a NATO exercise with fewer units," said Caldwell, "or just didn't go anywhere."

Admiral Boyle continued to petition Ottawa for more funds and was not pleased when, in January 1975, Richardson announced that the government soon intended to make more "significant changes" in defence that "would not impair to a significant degree our ability to continue to ensure the maintenance of our sovereignty in the North, or in any region in Canada."[52] For the Navy these significant changes were:

loss of another 590 personnel;
loss of six Argus patrol aircraft;
no new ships, aircraft or men; and
insufficient funds to resume normal operations.

But there was one bright spot. Rear-Admiral Boyle would be promoted to the rank of vice-admiral in the summer. In Halifax, the admiral said he was "humbled" by his promotion but confided privately that he would just as soon stay a rear-admiral and keep his six Argus aircraft.

Boyle received some financial relief in the April 1, 1975 budget, but it was not enough. He had hoped to start the new fiscal year by resuming the one-third of normal operations which had been cut. His new budget was $65 million, or $7.5 million less than requested, so operational hours of ships and aircraft were set at 82 percent of "normal minimum requirements" for the rest of the year.

During this financial squeeze period the Navy also lost its two important forward-bases on the East Coast, closed down to save money for fuel. "We were forced to pull in our horns from our forward facilities at St. John's (Newfoundland) and our base at Frobisher (Baffin Island)," said Timbrell, "because we were broke." Both bases were pivotal resupply points for ships swinging North or out to the North Atlantic for prolonged periods. The base at St. John's had tugs, a fuel-tank farm equipped to refuel naval vessels and advance headquarters control facilities. Frobisher's small unit was an important fuel and repair stop for northern flights and provided immediate requirements for ships.

"Each closing was a pullback" that weakened the Navy's ability to operate in its own waters, said Timbrell, "and eventually you come to a point where you have to say, 'sorry, I cannot do it anymore!' . . . we're not far from that now."

In addition, Admiral Boyle received a not-unexpected Christmas message from Ottawa: he would not be getting his long-promised new headquarters building. A reporter described his present one as "old style . . . the wind almost whistles in one side and out the other when there is a good maritime gale."[53]

MARCOM headquarters is a squat red-brick building that lies half hidden from sight between railway tracks and the harbour. It is too small to house the admiral's staff, who are scattered in makeshift offices, many of pre-war vintage, across the city. During the blustery winter of 1974-75 while Admiral Boyle struggled to keep his Navy afloat, toiling into the early hours of the morning in a dimly lit (to cut hydro bills) office, he could not have been heartened to read the glowing description of the new $88 million French language training and recruit centre planned for CFB St. Jean. It is the most elaborate — and expensive — single defence building project ever undertaken by the Trudeau government.

FESTERING BOYLE

By the Spring of 1975 Admiral Boyle had become frazzled around the edges trying to juggle shrinking resources to meet expanding tasks. He was barking at his men, living up to his nickname "Festering," which he earned as a feisty sub-lieutenant because of his tendency to boil briefly before exploding when things were not done correctly. He had done everything humanly possible to fulfil his duty and he was worried because the government was not listening to his warnings about the growing Soviet naval menace off the coasts. On June 8, he finally blew up and after the dust had settled it was obvious he had damaged his chances to be named the next CDS.

During a routine briefing session in Halifax, Boyle became worked up and told a weekend caucus meeting of twenty-one Tory MPs: "Right now the resources we have to do the job are inadequate . . . if we can't put up then we should shut up and surrender our sovereignty to the Americans." Unfortunately for the candid admiral, reporters were present.

Boyle explained that he was having a difficult time coping

with a budget that was $7.5 million short of what he needed. To compensate, operational hours of ships and aircraft had been increased slightly from the previous year but were still running 18 percent below normal minimum requirements. Housekeeping restraints — such as doused lights and two-sided letters — had saved a few million but it was not enough.

"I took a stone, and got a vice, and I squeezed it until blood came out of it," he said. "There's nothing left for this year, and I can't save any more." To meet the Navy's payroll, Boyle dipped into the Command's $17 million fuel account — one of the few non-fixed budget items — and reduced the number of operational hours until $3.8 million was saved. "So instead of our ships being at sea 120 days a year," he said, "they are now at sea 90 days. And instead of flying for 437 hours a month, our aircraft are now flying 365 hours. The difference is the saving of $3.8 million."[54]

But such reductions, he warned, made it difficult for the Navy to keep an eye on Soviet activities in Canadian waters, which he noted were increasing at an alarming rate. "I do need your understanding and help," he told the delighted Tories, "and hope that you can all speak with one voice in urging the Government to provide the Department of National Defence with the resources to do the job."[55]

Before he was finished, Boyle accused the government of "falling down on defence commitments to allies . . . every time I go down to the United States I hang my head in shame," and expressed amazement that the environment department was spending $30 million on two coastal patrol boats while "I have destroyers tied up at the seawall that can't put out to sea because I don't have enough money for fuel."

Boyle was summoned to Ottawa to explain his remarks, but no disciplinary action was taken. Instead, Richardson glossed the affair by commending Boyle's "excellent statement . . . the kind of factual information that should be more widely known by the Canadian public."[56] Bloodied but unbowed, Boyle returned to Halifax confident that he had done his duty. "My job is to serve my master," he said during his outburst, "but I also believe it's somebody's job to inform the Canadian public of what the threat is." An aide explained later: "The Admiral is not a calculating man. He thought he was just giving some honest answers to some honest questions." Two years later Boyle would be forced into early retirement, on orders from the Prime Minister's office.

Through 1975 and into the Spring of the following year operational patrols remained 18 to 20 percent below normal. One NATO exercise was missed, Arctic surveillance flights were spaced up to three weeks apart and some essential weapons training was scrapped altogether. The situation would finally cause General Dextraze to blurt: "Our warships haven't fired their bloody guns in two years. How long can you remain professional by just watching others."[57]

A budget increase of 10 percent in April 1976 allowed the Navy to resume normal sea and air patrols for the first time in three years. A Navy League report indicates just how paralysed the Navy's operations were: "Sovereignty operations on the East Coast alone in 1976 required more than 260 ship days at sea, in addition to a minimum of two Argus long-range patrols (coastal or Arctic) per week and with a major portion of Tracker aircraft engaged on surveillance patrols in the same area. This represented *twice* the level of sovereignty and surveillance operations in 1975."

On the West Coast, "these operations were repeated on a smaller scale . . . but the increase in the sovereignty and surveillance contribution for the year on that coast was *five times the level of the previous year.*"[58]

Modest budget increases made it possible for the Navy to continue surveillance patrols on a more or less regular basis, although in 1976 Admiral Boyle was forced to cut them back by 10 percent to give his overworked crews a rest. Resumption of normal patrols also threw a great strain on the aging fleet and in 1976 Boyle admitted that increased operational demands had forced him to extend routine refitting of his sixteen steam-powered destroyers from twenty to forty-eight months, which exceeds safety limits.[59] Next to a dwindling number of serviceable ships, manpower has become the admiral's number one headache.

MANPOWER SHORTAGE

Today Admiral Collier does not have enough men to crew his ships and those he does have are so overworked that they leave the service, which further aggravates the problem. From 1969 to 1978, partly because of forced personnel reductions, the Navy's manpower plunged from 17,000 officers and men to 9,500, while crewing requirements remained about the same and operational requirements increased. It's a vicious circle which saw the admiral press into service fifty-four sea cadets and two hundred Naval reservists in February 1977, so his East Coast ships could participate in annual spring exercises off Puerto Rico. Without this infusion of semi-skilled manpower at least one ship would have to stay home.

In fact, says Caldwell, MARCOM "was only able to keep two ships in operation during 1977 because they were using reserves and Sea Cadets." And while most cadets found deep-sea adventure fascinating, there were some ugly results from being forced to use children aboard ships. In December 1977, for example, fourteen-year-old Sea Cadet Louise Henriouelle of Port Hardy, B.C., lost her leg while working in the engine room of the MV Wildwood, a twelve-metre search-and-rescue vessel operated by CFB Holberg. While the craft was bouncing around in choppy seas off the north coast of Vancouver Island, Louise slipped and caught her leg in the boat's propeller shaft.[60]

In 1976 the Navy's manpower shortage was so acute that the government had to renege on its pre-unification deal that men from one service would not be sent to service in another against their will and began drafting air force helicopter crews to ships. "It has become nearly impossible," said Commodore Glenn Rosenroll in Halifax, to run the helicopter destroyers properly because of a shortage of sea-based helicopter pilots and maintenance men.[61]

In January 1977 General Dextraze underscored the problem: "A minimum of 900 personnel in Maritime Command is urgently needed to maintain our present level of operation, and allow the sailor some hope for a quasi-normal family life." He added: "The ships are seldom in port, the crews hard pressed, hence attrition is mounting. A minimum increase of 10 percent of all hard sea positions . . . *is not only warranted but is absolutely necessary if we are to carry out our assigned missions.*"[62]

Privately, however, naval officers say they need a minimum of 2,000 men to bring the proper 60-40 ratio back into line. The 900 men Dextraze refers to, they point out, are technical specialists, the men who make or break the Navy in today's electronic world. "The ratio (at sea) is 80-20 for most of them, and for some senior specialists it is literally 100 per cent to nothing," said one senior admiral. "What does it do to them? What does it mean to their marriages? It drives more and more to quit and our problems worsen. All the new ships in the world aren't worth anything if we can't fix that."[63]

Finally, in July 1977, Defence Minister Danson offered the Navy some hope. He announced a general 4,700-man increase in strength for the total forces, of which the Navy would receive only 600 over the next few years. In reality, it is only a paper increase because statistics show that for every 100 men who join the Navy, 72 quit — or are discharged — within the first five years. This year the Admiral will be lucky to get another 200 men. And his operational problems are not confined to the sea — they extend to his small fleet of patrol aircraft which, like the ships, are being held together by baling wire and love.

**PLANES**
Between 1969 and 1977 the strength of the naval air arm declined from seventy-one to fourty-four fixed-wing patrol aircraft, while its area of surveillance doubled. The planes are now responsible for patrolling close to six million square miles of ocean and ice — or about 135,000 square miles apiece. For a handful of twenty-year-old propeller-driven aircraft and their crews, it's quite a challenge.

The Maritime Air Group (MAG) is an integral part of the Navy's over-all surveillance capability. But in fact it is no longer naval. In September 1975, the naval air arm was absorbed by the newly created Air Command, and MAG was born. The logic was simple: anything with wings belonged to the resurrected air force. The group is responsible for management of all air resources engaged in maritime patrol and surveillance, and provides ASW aircraft as part of Canada's contribution to NATO. Operational control of the group remains with MARCOM while its aircraft are carrying out maritime missions.

Today, far-ranging surveillance flights and ASW patrols above Canada's three coastlines are handled by MAG's twenty-six four-engine Argus LRPAs, which fly from squadron at Greenwood, N.S., Summerside, P.E.I. and Comox, B.C. The six Argus removed from service at Greenwood in June 1975 as part of the general defence cutback, are now being cannibalized to keep their wing-weary brethren aloft.

Short-range coastal patrols are flown by eighteen twin-engine

Trackers, those venerable refugees from Bonaventure whose remarkable cruising speed of 160 m.p.h. gives them just enough range to make one frantic circuit of the 200 mile limit before heading home. Aside from being painfully slow, the Trackers were until quite recently blind. In the mid-1970s, as part of the government's modernization program, the Trackers lost their newly installed electronic ASW gear. The reason: not enough aviation technicians to maintain it. Rendered deaf, dumb and electronically blind to the presence of subs (or surface vessels on cloudy days), the Trackers were of little value as a patrol plane. In 1976, however, the government reversed its plan to scrap the Trackers and declared they would continue coastal patrols until at least 1985. To help them along, the forces have since spent $11.5 million to restore and upgrade the Trackers' radar and navigational equipment. Until then it was so inadequate that Trackers were not permitted to use transport ministry airports.[64]

During the early 1970s the Navy's top priority was obtaining a replacement aircraft for the venerable Argus, whose aging avionics systems were next to useless for detecting nuclear submarines. Finally, in July 1976, after five years of political wrangling and delay, the government ordered eighteen new Lockheed Aurora LRPAs for a contract price of $1.03 billion, the biggest single defence purchase in Canada's peacetime history. The eighteen Auroras are scheduled to replace the twenty-six Argus between 1980 and 1981.

More than one defence critic and military man has wondered how eighteen turbo-prop Auroras are going to replace twenty-six Argus. Admiral Boyle considered twenty-five new planes to be the Navy's minimum requirement; Admiral Timbrell swore by thirty-six. A highly placed DND source confirmed that twenty-five was the "buy" figure until inflation and bureaucratic delays pushed the project price over a billion dollars. So the number was dropped to eighteen.

Meanwhile, the Argus-Tracker patrol team, a case of the lame leading the blind, will soldier on as the Navy's aerial watchdogs until at least 1981. The Trackers are reasonably effective on sunny days for spotting fishing boats for the fisheries department and geese and caribou for environment. The Argus have their problems, too. At a time when Soviet nuclear submarines are rated as the greatest threat to Canada, it is less than reassuring to hear that a feature of the Argus' detection system is its "radar exhaust trail indicator, which gives the ability to detect diesel exhaust trails" of conventional submarines.[65]

Viewed from afar, a Navy of twenty-six warships, forty-four old patrol planes and 9,500 men appears more like a remnant from the past than a guardian of the future. How well can they perform their primary role as guardians of maritime sovereignty? The following incident suggests they do it with great difficulty.

### RED FACES IN THE NORTH

Canada's loud claims to sovereignty of disputed northern seas and territories seemed mostly rhetorical in late August 1975, when a game little Polish yacht kept the Navy running in Arctic circles for three days. The eighty-foot Gedania, in defiance of a government order, slipped in and out of the Northwest Passage and vanished into the headlines, despite an intensive air/sea search to find her.

Her daring voyage into Canada's backyard, after twice being refused permission by External Affairs, was an expensive embarrassment to Admiral Boyle, and showed just how weak the Navy's northern shield really was. How had Gedania been missed? "The yacht made its way through the passage," a naval spokesman admitted, "during a week when there were no flights over the Arctic."

Gedania's captain claimed the whole thing was just an "adventure." Dariusz Bogucki decided to ignore External's orders because it would be his only chance to follow in the path of his polar hero, Norway's Roald Amundsen, who had navigated the passage at the turn of the century. The naval supply ship Protecteur reported seeing the yacht enter Lancaster Sound at the eastern end of the passage, but little notice was taken of its routine sighting report because External had failed to inform the Navy of its earlier decisions.

It was only after Gedania's crew of ten came ashore at Resolute on the southern tip of Cornwallis Island, 350 miles inside the passage, that government officials realized the ship was there illegally and ordered her out of Canadian waters. After taking on supplies the Gedania headed east and vanished.

Following press reports of the plucky little ship's adventure, the Navy was ordered to find Gedania and escort her to international waters. But the Navy could not find Gedania, despite three days of searching by ships and two Argus aircraft. The search was called off on September 6 after Greenland radio reported that Gedania had provisioned at Thule on September 2 and was heading for St. John's, Newfoundland.

"There is no excuse," complained one newspaper, "other than the ruinous defence policy of recent years, for the Gedania reaching Resolute undetected. Nor is there excuse for her being able thereafter to escape surveillance."[66]

When External refused to make an official protest to the Polish embassy, dismissing the defiance of a government order as "not a great issue in Polish-Canadian relations," one respected defence writer said: "It is hard to understand how . . . the movements in sensitive Canadian waters of a vessel based and registered in a Communist state — one partially occupied by Soviet troops — can be regarded with such equanimity by federal authorities. Has East-West détente really carried us so far?"[67] One defence spokesman acknowledged that "if the crew members don't have sophisticated monitoring devices to work with, they certainly have eyes, logs and notebooks."[68] In Ottawa, visiting U.S. Admiral Isaac Kidd, SACLANT himself, was annoyed and answered a flat "yes" when asked if he was concerned that a Soviet ship could voyage undetected into the continent's backyard.[69]

In addition, the Gedania chase cost the Navy more than $200,000 in fuel. A naval spokesman said that in order to balance MARCOM's stretched fuel budget, two or three Arctic patrols, or ten coastal patrols would not be flown.[70]

Besides the monetary loss, the Gedania incident was not a morale booster for the hard pressed fleet. "Even the youngest seaman knows when we're putting up a great facade and can't meet our commitments," said Admiral Timbrell. "When he knows it, and knows he has to live with it, and then it's rubbed down his nose because one little Polish ship slips in and makes fun of us for four days because we can't find her, it hurts like hell. It kicks hell out of his morale."

Timbrell and other senior naval officers believe the Gedania incident would never have happened had the Navy been adequately equipped and not starved for fuel to maintain its regular coastal patrols.

Tory MP Patrick Nowlan (Annapolis Valley) called the infrequent sovereignty flights a "charade," adding scornfully that if the Navy could no longer monitor the movements of a yacht known to be in Canadian waters, "I wonder where other ships and foreign objects are."[71]

### GOING DOWN

The Navy of 1978 is closer to the wrecking yards than most people realize. That's the verdict of four recently retired admirals who decided to break the traditional code of silence and tell Canadians why their Navy was sinking at home and to warn of the consequences of failing to contribute a fair share to collective defence.

As the nation's top seagoing brass when they retired in 1975, their remarks validate much criticism of Trudeau's maritime defence policies, confirming, at least, that the fleet in which they served is no longer seaworthy. The admirals all spoke out in the March 1976 edition of *Canadian Shipping:*[72]

"Of all the governments we've had," said Vice-Admiral J.C. O'Brien, "the one that has mentioned the word priorities most, and considered Canada's defence least, is the Trudeau government."

O'Brien, who was commandant of the NATO Defence College in Rome before retiring, warned that "it is vital for us to invest in a strong Navy . . . because over the next ten years, as raw materials dry up, I expect to see an intense struggle for the possession and control of these materials."

The rise of the Red Navy, he pointed out, "is the traditional method of expansion — a strong fleet, a forward base," and so on. "In light of Soviet naval expansion, we must anticipate confrontations all around the world."

But at home, he said, "I see our Navy being starved to death because Canada has abdicated its responsibility of maintaining a self-sufficient industrial base from which to produce the necessary equipment." O'Brien claimed Trudeau's obsession with "social services, upon which inordinate sums are being spent —even squandered," and his patent "neglect of the defence establishment has annoyed NATO . . . and the Americans."

Rear-Admiral R.H. Leir chided the government for not amalgamating Canada's several navies,* which "are splintered

*In number of ships, the Navy is considerably smaller than the combined fleets of the Coast Guard, RCMP, and federal departments of transport, environment and Fisheries.

among many government departments in a most Gilbert and Sullivan manner."

Leir, who retired as Chief of Maritime Operations at NDHQ, cited many examples of wasteful duplication in maritime training and resources and suggested the Navy's future role in the defence of North America be directed toward "surveillance of our water and air spaces," leaving the military back-up to the Americans.

"The next best thing to going out there and punching them on the nose is to tell the world they're there," he said, "and ask somebody else to punch them for us." Canadians may not like the idea of leaving the punching to the Americans, he added, but in light of the fact "that Canada doesn't have the economic base to have its own fleet of A-subs, it is a rational answer, no matter how unpopular." He favours using hydrofoils for coastal patrol work. But first "we do have to stop freeloading and start paying our own way."

Whither the Navy? "We should guard jealously this shrinking body of expertise," he said. "If it remains free of bureaucratic interference, it will serve the country well."

All may be quiet on the western front, but the "yacht squadron" will have to face "an emerging Red Chinese Navy" in the Pacific fairly soon, warned Rear-Admiral R.J. Pickford, who retired as Commander of MARPAC. And they will have to do it "without the powerful help, politically and practically, of a NATO alliance."

Delays in building replacement ships for the fleet had seriously hurt Canadian industry, he claimed, adding that "we now have some serious catching up to do as a large percentage of our fleet approaches obsolescence with no replacements in sight."

Canada's 200-mile zone "will never be fully effective until we have the ships to make it so," he said, pointing out that it was not unreasonable to ask "that our Navy . . . be maintained at an adequate level to discharge all the tasks asked of it today, and which will certainly be asked of it tomorrow."

Admiral Timbrell was mildly caustic: "In Canada, with our clear announcements that sovereignty/defence of the homeland and NATO are the principal declarations for our security, then one cannot but wonder why the government has failed to provide sufficient funds so that the forces, particularly the Navy, are able to carry out their necessary duties effectively." Détente, he said, is a smokescreen for a menacing Soviet naval build-up and he hoped government would not be "lulled into a state of unpreparedness and thereby abandon our obligations to the future."

The following chart paints a bleak picture of a destroyer fleet which is close to the end of its operational life. Twenty years is considered to be the initial lifespan of a modern warship; twenty-five is the maximum before obsolescence and decay overtakes it. Not included are the three relatively new supply ships, which should be good into the 1990s. With no new warships on the horizon, Admiral Collier's Navy shapes up like this:

**Warship Fleet**

| Ships | Age | Coast E | Coast W |
|---|---|---|---|
| 4 Tribals ........................................ 1 ..... | | 4 | |
| 2 Annapolis DDHs.............. 1 ..... | | 2 | |
| 6 St. Laurents DDHs* ...... 1 ..... | | 6 | |
| 4 Restigouche DDEs ....... 1 ..... (improved) | | | 4 |
| 4 Mackenzie DDEs ............. 1 ..... | | | 4 |
| 3 Restigouche DDEs** ..... 1 .... | | 1 | 2 |
| 3 "Oberon" subs ............... 1 ..... | | 3 | |

'76    81    86    91    96    (16) (10)

20 years: .... 25 years: ......

*The St. Laurents have already passed their useful lifespan because of greater stress and wear on their hulls caused by their latter-day conversion to DDHs from DDEs.

**The three Restigouche ships are in reserve and would require extensive refitting to be fit for sea duty.

## THE FUTURE

If present government plans for the partial renewal of the fleet are carried through, the Navy will cease to exist as a meaningful military force within a decade. The announcement last December that Cabinet will spend $63 million to merely explore the specifics of building six new destroyers over the next ten years was at best a reprieve for the hope that Canada will meet her maritime responsibilities for the future.

In 1976, with most of the Navy's warships reaching the end of their operational lives, Cabinet was prodded into considering a naval building program. Requests from admirals Boyle and Timbrell and General Dextraze for action had been rejected several times as too costly, but Richardson finally convinced his colleagues that time was running out. Action was needed now, he said, because eight years was the normal lead time required to get a warship off the drawing boards and into the fleet, and the fleet was getting long in the tooth. In his memo to Cabinet he pointed out just what bad shape it was in:

> The oldest ships in our operational surface fleet will reach thirty years and be no longer either effective or maintainable, by about 1983, and others will follow through the remainder of the decade and into the 1990's.
>
> Because of the long lead time for warship construction it will be necessary for the government in 1976 to address a plan for ship replacement. Such a plan, identifying types and numbers of ships to be procured as the present inventory gradually phases out, is essential to effective management of the defence budget.

Finally, on January 13, 1977, Vice-Admiral Falls announced details of the long-awaited ship replacement program to delegates attending the annual Conference of Defence Associations (CDA), in Ottawa. Naval brass poured into the Chateau Laurier's chandeliered Adam Room expecting to hear the clink of keels being laid down that afternoon. They were in for a shock.

Falls told them the government intended to build twenty general-purpose patrol frigates. However, because of financial restraints, they would have to be phased in over twenty years at a cost of $3.5 billion in 1977 funds. The first ships would not come into service until the mid-1980s but all should be in place by the early 1990's.[73] Boyle and other naval men did not like the plan, claiming that a navy of twenty frigates and a handful of aged Tribals would be little more than a coast guard. Plainly annoyed, Boyle delivered his talk on the growing Soviet naval menace then slipped home to Halifax on a late plane, sending apologies to General Dextraze for missing the chief's annual dinner to honour the nation's top military commanders.

Within days of the announcement naval planners and industry representatives began working on design criteria for the new frigates, submitting them to Cabinet in the Spring. Key contracts for prototype ships were to be signed by late 1979 and both parties anxiously awaited Cabinet's decision. Silence. With the departure of Richardson, the program's champion, Cabinet was again divided on the need for twenty ships, so a fateful compromise was struck. Danson announced it on December 22.

Instead of building twenty ships to form the nucleus of a new Navy, the government could only afford to build — or consider building — six, just enough to replace the decrepit St. Laurent DDHs. The six would cost $1.5 billion — a staggering $250 million apiece — in 1977 dollars, considerably less than the $3.5 billion previously earmarked for the twenty frigates.[74] The price is a shocker because other navies can build modern destroyers of similar design for about $40 million a copy. Last year defence officials estimated new ships would cost about $125 million each, but that was for a series of twenty ships and numbers reduce cost. What will the Navy get for a quarter of a billion dollars apiece?

Specifics are still to be worked out but the new ship will be smaller than a Tribal, weighing between 3,500 to 4,000 tons and carrying one helicopter instead of two. Naval sources speculate it will be closer to 3,500 tons and possibly built around the proven 371-foot hull of the Annapolis class destroyers.

The ship is expected to carry: anti-submarine torpedoes; short to medium-range anti-aircraft missiles; medium-range anti-ship missiles; a rapid fire, light calibre gun; a complex electronic counter-measure system to jam and decoy enemy electrical systems.[75]

Construction of the first new ship is scheduled to start in 1981. It would be finished in 1985, and the follow-on ships phased into service by the end of the decade. Danson called the patrol frigate program the "first stage" of an ongoing replacement plan, but top-ranking naval officers fear stage two will never materialize.

Until the new frigates arrive, Danson added, several of the Navy's old steam-driven destroyers would be modernized under the Destroyer Life Extension Program in order to keep them "operating safely and usefully over their remaining life span." This is, at best, a wasteful stop-gap measure. In response to Danson's remarkable claim, noted defence writer Peter Ward of Ottawa, wrote: "a warship's effective life is twenty-five years and claims that usefulness can be extended to thirty years are largely cosmetic. By the time the six ships now under construction are operating — 1989 at the earliest — every ship presently in service, except the DDH-280s, will be ready for the breaker's yards."[76]

Commodore Caldwell agrees. Refitting the old ships is "just money down the drain, tens of millions of dollars worth . . . it would be better spent on new ships, then we'd have something that would be effective for a long time." The first ships resurrected under the program probably would be the trio of mothballed DDEs, St. Croix, Chaudiere and Columbia, followed by the Restigouche class. Caldwell believes the first three could be made "reasonably effective" for routine duties. But the man responsible for the job is not so sure.

In November 1977, Commodore Ray Ross, Director-General of DND's Maritime Engineering and Maintenance section, told a meeting of engineers that it would be extremely difficult to upgrade the combat effectiveness of the old ships because they belonged to an age of bygone technology. In many cases key spare parts were impossible to obtain because they were no longer being made.

New technology needed to be incorporated into the ships, which meant considerable overhauling and redesigning. And what would happen should the modernized ships require spares and parts no longer available? The ships had already been refurbished once to keep them going beyond their normal lifespan. The cost of doing it a second time was going to be high. Ross could not give a price for the work, but cautioned the engineers that the impact on Canadian industry "should not be underestimated."[77] The engineers had only one question for Ross: after they had assembled design teams and finished the job, would there be any more work?

The same fear haunts the work-starved Canadian shipbuilding industry which is anxious to build the new frigates. Two consortia of yards from across the country are competing for the contracts. The challenge is more considerable this time because, unlike past programs when the yards just built the ships, industry has been asked to *design* them as well. A few years ago the Navy could have designed its own ships as it had always done in the past, but it recently lost the know-how. According to Commodore Thomas Arnott, head of the frigate program, economic restraints of the past few years forced the Navy to scrap its ship design section, with a regrettable loss of naval engineering expertise.[78] Between 1974 and 1975 the engineering team at NDHQ which designed the Tribals scattered to the winds. Now that job will fall to private industry, if they care to take it on.

The group winning the contract will find itself left with the expertise and the capital necessary to compete aggressively in international shipbuilding when the Canadian program is finished. And that's what bothers shipbuilders. Without the prospect of continued naval construction, both industry and the Navy will find themselves on a downhill course. It is more economical by far to keep the yards working regularly than to run the industry on a boom-or-bust basis.

Ideally, Canada should be constructing two new warships a year until the fleet is equipped with twenty or more modern warships. Then a construction program should be designed to maintain the naval strength chosen by the politicians. A long-range program would bring stability back to a vital industry and guarantee the Navy a steady supply of ships and maintenance support.[79]

THE TRIBAL ALTERNATIVE

Ironically, while Ottawa considers a new type of ship for the Navy, there is a comparatively cheap option that could keep the fleet strong and provide work for ailing shipyards. Build more DDH-280 Tribal destroyers. The benefits are legion.

NATO commanders rate the Canadian-built Tribal as the best warship, pound for pound, in the western world. An important plus for the Tribal is that it possesses the clout and size required to work on the high seas with NATO. The ships also carry two Sea King combat-capable helicopters — the only medium-sized warship in the world that does — which, in the designer's own words, "effectively extend the vessel's underwater surveillance and attack capability."[80] The new patrol frigate would carry only one helicopter, a limitation the Tribals were designed to overcome. When the need for aerial surveillance of maritime areas has never been greater, noted Caldwell, the second helicopter "more than doubles aerial operations, with little or no increase in the ships' helicopter-handling and maintenance."[81] The move to one helicopter "is a mistaken economy measure."

Some of the Tribals' strong points are worth noting. Unlike conventionally-powered steam destroyers, which require refitting every two years, Tribals can go ten years between refits with just routine maintenance. They were the first warships in the world to use gas turbine rather than steam plants for propulsion. "Think of this for action," said Admiral Boyle in 1976, "upon pressing a button on the bridge to ignite the main engines, you find that ninety-six seconds later you're doing twenty-five knots through the water and still accelerating."[82] His other ships take four hours to warm up before sailing.

Tribals are the envy of other navies, including the American, which sent a team of designers to Halifax a few years ago to ogle them. In 1976, Captain A.G. Sigmond, USN, retiring Commodore of the NATO Standing Naval Force, praised the Tribals as the best ships in the international flotilla. "I have always given the 280 the opportunity to act as a 'show window' to demonstrate to the rest what this gas turbine ship can do." With her ability to "lay to" (drift silently without power) for extended periods and then flash into action, he said, "I would like to think we have caught our quarry (training submarine) by surprise once or twice."[83] Tribal captains love their ships, too.

On February 15, 1977, Captain G.L. Edwards of HMCS Algonquin told a meeting of engineers the Tribals have now collectively operated twelve years covering over 376,000 miles, and have operated in all sea conditions from arctic to tropical. His assessment: "They are first among the finest ships in NATO and, in many ways, perhaps the world." Edwards rated the propulsion system as the best in the world and virtually trouble free. Aside from a few minor structural problems that could be corrected in later models, Edwards concluded that the Tribals have shown that Canada is capable of producing highly successful ships which are the envy of all other navies — including the Soviet — and should continue to design and build her own warships.[84]

W.H. German, a leading Canadian marine consultant and naval architect, wrote: "the Tribals have proven to be the most trouble-free vessels the Navy has ever had, with remarkable ship handling characteristics and excellent fuel economy." A repeat order for them, "modified only to satisfy new requirements for sensors, weaponry and communications, and with modest ice capabilities . . . would provide the Canadian Forces with a first-class weapon system much earlier than could be done in any other way, but at a comparatively lesser cost."[85]

The initial Tribal building program absorbed the design and development costs, and experts believe another ten could be built in the next several years for less than $2 billion 1977 dollars. Such a program would probably cost no more than the proposed patrol frigate undertaking, and has the advantage of producing more ships in less time to replace rapidly failing destroyers. And of course a Tribal building program would pump desperately needed orders into Canada's faltering shipbuilding industries.

In addition, recent developments in shipboard electronics have made the Tribals almost as cheap to crew as a frigate, a fact which prompted a small group of pro-Tribal officers to try and get a few more built before the frigate program was launched. They pointed out that a frigate with a crew of 180 represents, at today's rates of pay, a daily payroll of about $2,500, or about $1,500 less than a 280-man Tribal. However, the introduction of advanced technology into modernized Tribals, such as solid state electronics for main machinery control — earmarked for the frigates — could reduce their crew requirements by 15 to 20 percent, or at least forty men. This means that ten new Tribals with crews of 240 each would cost about $3.3 million a year more to crew (600 extra men) than ten frigates with crews of 180 each.

Surprisingly, Defence Minister Barney Danson made the best case for re-equipping the Navy with modernized Tribals. In January 1977, during his first visit to MARCOM headquarters, Danson was asked if he thought a vessel as costly and sophisticated as the Tribal should be used for fisheries patrol. "Yes I do," he replied. "It is an expensive fisheries patrol vessel but it is also a fighting vessel and this is the multi-tasking we have to do . . . At this time it's able to serve that role well and fulfil its other responsibilities, especially in NATO — *and we can't fulfil our NATO responsibilities with a fisheries patrol vessel.*"[86] A month later Danson suggested Canada could benefit economically by building and selling Tribals to allied navies, leaving room for speculation that Ottawa would just as soon sell its best piece of military hardware abroad before equipping its own Navy with it. "Our DDH-280 destroyers are the best value, the best piece of equipment that exists. Perhaps we should be making those and letting someone else make something else for us."[87]

The question arises that if Tribals are such a superior ship, why is Cabinet opting for an expensive long-range plan to produce untried mini-Tribals? The answer is, DND officials readily acknowledge, to save money in the short run and keep future naval manpower requirements down to a minimum.

First, the financial impact of a long-range program can be cushioned over many years, where a Tribal building program would require immediate funds. "Shipyards could start cutting steel tomorrow," notes Caldwell. In the next decade the defence budget is already committed to spending billions for Auroras, tanks and new jet fighters. It could not stand the shock of a multi-billion dollar shipbuilding program for several years, so new ships were pushed far into the future.

Second, the proposed frigate will require a crew of between 170 and 190, in comparison to a second-generation Tribal's 240. "The decreased crew size," notes the *Financial Post*, "will be stipulated to designers because Maritime Command is already having a hard time finding enough crew members to man the present vessels."[88]

WHAT THE NAVY NEEDS

Canada needs a Navy that can perform the roles assigned to it by the government. These are known: protection of sovereignty, which means constant surveillance of coastlines and our new 200-mile offshore economic zone; patrolling the Arctic clear to the Pole, which will help Canada's disputed claims to much of the area; and contributing to collective defence of the West by keeping watch on the vital North Atlantic sea lanes as a member of NATO.

Canadian geography makes it mandatory that we contribute to the protection of the strategic nuclear deterrent by surveillance of Soviet submarines in the Atlantic, Arctic and Pacific approaches to the continential U.S. In all, the Navy must have enough resources to adequately patrol six million square miles of ocean and ice. To do this Canada needs to develop a "balanced" Navy.

The forced economies of the Trudeau period forced Canada into building a Navy with one predominant ship — the destroyer. Our submarines exist primarily to train destroyer crews. Fleet supply ships exist to keep destroyers at sea longer. We do not have an aircraft carrier because it was too costly to fuel and maintain her 1,100 man crew, who were needed to man the new Tribals. Our minesweepers and tiny Gate vessels are used for reserve training. The fleet lacks a smaller warship (the Bras d'Or?) for patrolling the 200-mile limit. All in all, Canada's Navy is anything but balanced, which places severe limitations on what Admiral Collier can effectively handle.

The Arctic provides a good example of why the Navy needs more balanced components. Although responsible for maintaining northern sovereignty, the Navy has no warships capable of operating above the 60th parallel except in summer, and then only as far as Baffin Island. Naval ships proceeding north at other times require the help of ice-breakers, which belong to other government departments. The Navy needs some of its own, possibly two. The LRPA is the most efficient and economical means of keeping the Arctic under surveillance, and more than one should be flying at all times. The current once-a-month flights are totally inadequate. And to be truly effective, the LRPAs should be backed up with underwater sonar gear for detection of submarines. There is also a crying need for re-opening an Arctic military base to handle ships and aircraft on northern patrol. Financial restraints forced the Navy to close its advance base at Frobisher and something like it should be developed. Creation of the Northern Region headquarters at Yellowknife in the early 1970s was more a token "show the flag" effort than a determined move to put some military muscle in the Arctic.

According to Admiral Timbrell Canada needs a "combat capable" Navy because such a force is capable of performing during peacetime or war. It is also the best bargain because by guarding the sea lanes, adds Timbrell, "Canada can make her most effective maritime contribution to NATO and with these same contributions, meet her sovereignty/defence of the homeland commitments."[89] We get two for the price of one.

Richardson, too, in his memo to Cabinet, stressed that Canada required "a combat capable Navy," because "to operate at all in a situation of hostilities involving Canada and the Soviet Union, even to carry out patrol off our own coasts, our maritime forces would require effective self-defence capabilities, involving, specifically, capabilities to detect, identify, track and destroy submarines, and at least some capability to defend against attack by submarine launched cruise missile."

Pointing out the advantages of maintaining a flexible Navy with sharp teeth, Richardson added: "if our forces have ships and aircraft with combat capabilities ... including effective ASW capabilities, they will be able to undertake any of the range of possible maritime tasks, across the spectrum from surveillance and control of our coastal approaches against threats to our sovereignty, through detection and tracking of either attack or ballistic missile submarines in peacetime, to the protection of shipping in combat situations." In short, a Navy capable of fulfilling the tasks assigned without undue hardship and one with a fair chance of staying alive.

Failure to maintain a strong Navy, he warned, "would mean the effective abolition of our Navy in the common sense of the term as a combat arm, a decision which would surely create major political problems domestically." A smaller, weaker force "could not responsibily be ordered to sea at a time when hostilities involving the Soviet Union had broken out or appeared imminent, and hence could not contribute in any direct sense to deterrence or be considered an effective contribution to NATO."

In 1977 Admiral Timbrell, with help from naval sources in Ottawa, identified the kind of Navy Canada would need to meet its future maritime responsibilities.[90] Several top-ranking naval men were asked what they thought of it. Opinions ranged from "reasonable" to "adequate," but none thought it to be outlandish or unrealistic — or too expensive.

Timbrell's Navy is about twice the size of the present one in both ships and men. He calls for 22,000 seagoing officers and men, with an additional 6,000 in the air group. While this appears to be quite an increase, it merely puts the Navy's strength back to where it was about fifteen years ago, when it boasted more than sixty ships — everything from a carrier and escorts to minesweepers — and 20,000 men, and when it was responsible for about half the territory of today's Navy.

Timbrell's Navy shapes up like this:

Destroyers: 36, equipped to combat submarine and air threat, and with sufficient range to cross the Atlantic and operate in "brash"ice

Minesweepers: 12

Submarines: 10, equipped to detect and destroy enemy submarines and able to operate under ice

Supply ships: 4

Helicopters: 10

Missing from Timbrell's equation is a fleet of small ships for routine patrolling of the 200 mile limit. Cheaper and faster than destroyers, such a fleet — probably hydrofoils — is considered by many to be an essential component of a new Navy.

Does Canada really need thirty destroyers? It does, according to Admiral Falls. In March 1977 he told journalist Peter Cale: "When we add up the number of days that must be spent at sea to honour our commitments to NATO, to conduct fisheries protection and surveillance, and then to allow for maintenance cycles, the answer comes to about thirty destroyers, not twenty . . . In fact, had the government not decided to inject more money into capital replacements, *within a few years we would not just be weak, we'd be helpless."* [91] Falls, of course, was talking about Cabinet's decision to build twenty frigates, not six.

On the air side of the new Navy's ledger, Timbrell recommends a larger role for the tiny Maritime Air Group. He has argued for years that thirty-six Aurora LRPAs are required, not eighteen, and that immediate steps be taken to acquire a fleet of forty medium-range patrol aircraft to replace the useless Trackers. Both the Auroras and the potential Tracker replacement should also be equipped to "kill" surface ships and submarines. The new Auroras will lack such ability, by Cabinet direction, which means Canada is not getting much bang for its billion bucks. As it is, when the stingless Auroras replace the twenty-six Argus by 1981, the Navy's over-all surveillance capability will not have improved significantly.

The Aurora is a better aircraft than its rickety predecessor, but aside from turbo-props and a modern avionics system, it is of the same mid-fifties generation as the Argus and similar in general flight performance. The big improvement is in lower maintenance costs and improved detection capability. In short, eighteen propellor-driven aircraft, no matter how good electronically, will have a tough job covering the same amount of territory as twenty-six similar propellor-driven aircraft.

In 1977 Admiral Boyle explained just how important his patrol aircraft are in covering his command's 5.8 million square miles of assigned territory, and why he needs more of them. "We have the clearly defined duty to patrol it and, if necessary, to defend against attack on it, over it and below it. To do this we need a fleet of patrol aircraft. As you know, the government has decided to buy a modern, fully equipped force of new Lockheed long-range Aurora, eighteen of them. That was a vital decision, but of course it isn't enough. There are only so many hours we can afford to fly them within our budget. So we need some shorter range aircraft as well to patrol closer to the shores, particularly the new 200 mile limit."[92]

Brigadier-General Harold Carswell, former commander of the

Air Group, admitted that maximum operation of the eighteen Auroras will permit only a 12 percent increase in general surveillance capability. "They'll allow us to fly 25,000 hours each year, compared to the 22,000 hours we can manage in the Argus." He also confirmed the Navy is getting an inferior aircraft for a vastly higher cost due to five years of snarled negotiations, caused mostly by a power struggle and clash of personalities between defence officials and their counterparts in industry, trade and commerce.

"As the struggle went on to hold prices, we dropped some key items," Carswell said. "One is special equipment to keep close watch looking ahead in arctic ice conditions. This is a type of radar that views ahead, rather like a searchlight, in the ice. This has to be left out," along with other items he could not reveal.[93] Admiral Timbrell has pointed out that once the Aurora's costly ground information processing installations are in place, more aircraft could be purchased — and handled by the ground stations — at a fraction of the total cost of the billion-dollar package.

When the Auroras finally join MAG, they will find themselves yoked to a handful of partially blind, broken-winded Tracker mules. The Navy needs a short-range plane but realizes chances of getting it are slim. In recent years Cabinet has been cool to suggestions to replace the Tracker with a fleet of DASH-7 STOL (Short Takeoff and Land) aircraft, produced by the financially-troubled de Havilland Aircraft of Toronto, in which the Government holds a controlling interest.

Some defence experts believe a fleet of DASH-7s mixed with Auroras would give the Navy a more versatile surveillance capability. One of them is author Richard Rohmer, former chief of the Air Reserve, recently promoted to Major-General of Canada's reserve forces. In a 1976 interview Rohmer outlined the benefits of teaming up a fleet of thirty to forty DASH-7s with Auroras. The Auroras could patrol over Polar Ice areas and far out to sea, leaving the DASH-7s to cover inshore areas and much of the North. Because of their ability to operate from gravel strips, Rohmer saw the DASH-7s flying patrols from northern bases such as Frobisher Bay, Fort Chimo and Yellowknife, where a few could be based. DASH-7s could also land in remote northern regions, if required, which the Aurora cannot. Such a combination would be a boost to Canadian industry as well as help the Navy to underscore Canada's disputed claims to the Arctic.

But regardless of what type of aircraft will eventually replace the Tracker, it appears certain that MAG will fly far into the 1980s with no "kill" capability and insufficient men and planes to police all three sides of the world's longest coastline. For thirty-six mismatched aircraft, that's a tall order.

### REQUIEM FOR THE NAVY

Canada's Navy is headed on a collision course with disaster, steered there by Trudeau's poorly devised naval policies. Today the numbers of men, ships and planes have sunk to their lowest point in more than twenty years, and prospects for tomorrow are even bleaker.

Richardson, in his memo to Cabinet, warned that Canada could pay dearly for letting its Navy decay any further. Aside from losing valuable "expertise" and "a considerable investment . . . in advanced technology," Canada would forfeit her claims to ocean sovereignty. "The U.S. would have to take over from Canada responsibility for military protection of the CANLANT and MARPAC areas which include the contiguous waters subject to Canadian national jurisdiction. In this connection it should be noted that the extensive (and rich) continental shelf of our eastern seaboard occupies a large portion of the CANLANT area." Sovereignty declarations without the means to back them up are meaningless.

Boyle also warned Ottawa: "Starting with the St. Laurent class of ships that pass the twenty-five-year-old stage in 1981," he said in 1977, "we have a fleet that will no longer be able to perform. It means that we either replace them, or we must tell NATO and the world that we can no longer carry out the job we have undertaken."[94]

It is clear that Canada needs more of the modern warships like the ones Cabinet is now considering if it is to meet its maritime responsibilities of the future. But it also needs a diversity of naval vessels the like of which have not been seen since the Pearson days. And it appears Trudeau is not prepared to provide them, although he has doubled the Navy's workload since coming to power. The six frigates destined for the fading fleet will arrive too late to do much good and they will be distinctly inferior to the larger Tribals because of the Cabinet's refusal to allow small increases in manpower to crew a second-generation of these excellent destroyers. For want of a few thousand more men, taxpayers are being asked to spend needless billions to build a glorified coast guard. In fact, it could be as high as $10 billion, a figure given by Danson in November 1977 when he was asked how much it would cost to replace the present fleet because they had waited so long.[95]

When Admiral Falls took over the forces' top job — the first sailor to hold it — naval officers looked to him to shore up the fleet. Since becoming CDS, however, Falls appears to have succumbed to political pressure to toe the party line and is no longer making waves. In fact, in what must have been a painful duty, one of his first assignments was to preside over the firing of Admiral Boyle, who was again making disquieting noises down east.

After two years of relative silence, Boyle was back in the news complaining about the wretched state of the Navy and telling anyone who would listen about the dangers posed to Canada by Russia's growing maritime might. When he started telling service club luncheons that Russia would start a world war by 1980, that was too much.[96] Soviet officials in Ottawa complained to Trudeau's office, and détente-minded bureaucrats wanted Boyle silenced. Falls was asked to do the job, so he offered his colleague a *fait accompli:* take a desk job in Ottawa counting stock, or resign. Boyle stepped down, preferring to go down still wearing a commander's hat. His untimely departure deprived Canada of its most experienced naval commander at a critical time and it sent a chill through the thinning naval ranks. Senior officers remember only too clearly the confusion and cut-backs which followed the firing of another champion, Admiral William Landymore, who went down fighting for his fleet at the height of the unification battle.

A few months after Boyle's firing, Falls began back-tracking on his earlier statements that Canada would need more naval muscle to cope with expected challenges to its maritime sovereignty in the future. In December 1977, he dismissed Admiral Timbrell's charges that the Navy already lacked sufficient men and ships to carry out its sovereignty protection role. It would take "quite a concerted effort on someone's part," said Falls, "to try to violate our sovereignty and to challenge our laws to such an extent we would need more than the existing fleet. I can't see that kind of situation developing."[97] Perhaps Falls and government officials have forgotten about the Polish yacht Gedania that laughed its way in and out of the Northwest Passage.

In the final analysis, says Peter Ward, "if nothing more is decided than to build those six new ships — for an average cost of $250 million in 1977 dollars — the verdict of history will be that the government acted too late, with too little, and at too high a cost. Our offshore interests in fisheries and sea-bed minerals could well become easy pickings for foreigners, and our reputation as a naval cream puff would be assured internationally."[98]

# 3 MOBILE COMMAND

The Canadian Army enjoys a well-deserved reputation for its professionalism, courage and devotion to duty. Whether called upon to storm Vimy Ridge, probe Hitler's Fortress Europe at Dieppe or sandbag raging rivers on the Canadian Prairies, the Army was always front and centre. But today it is weak, hemorrhaging slowly from wounds inflicted by Trudeau's defence policies. Unless things change, the Army could simply fade away in a few years, just like the proverbial old soldiers.

Mobile Command (MOBCOM) was created in 1965 when the major elements of the Army were teamed up with tactical air units to form the heart of Hellyer's "global-mobile" force, the sharp end of the army. The force was tasked to "maintain combat-ready land and tactical air forces capable of rapid deployment in circumstances ranging from service in the European theatre to United Nations peacekeeping operations."[1] This concept had been a principal rationale of unification and MOBCOM was equipped with an array of light, airportable armour and jet combat aircraft in readiness for its new mission.

In theory, Hellyer's peacekeeping would protect Canadian interests (sovereignty through world stability) by dousing brushfire wars around the globe before they could touch off a third world war. On the priority scale, this international peacekeeping ranked slightly ahead of Canada's next and biggest defence effort abroad, NATO.

MOBCOM was "responsible for the provision of a rotational brigade in Europe, and for training two additional airportable brigades designed for rapid deployment" to Europe or other trouble spots.[2]

In 1968 it formed the Canadian Airborne Regiment, later based at Edmonton, for duty in the North and as Canada's standby brigade assigned to reinforce NATO's northern flank (Norway and Denmark) in the event of war with the Warsaw Pact nations.

The Command's main priorities at this time reflected Canada's belief that collective security arrangements offered the best chance to prevent nuclear war in a world fraught with ideological feuds and the often violent birth pangs of Third World nations.

They underscored a continuing commitment to support NATO and the United Nations, the twin pillars of Canada's postwar foreign policy. Defence of North America was MOBCOM's last priority, because it was generally understood that any army's final role was to defend the homeland when all else had failed.

But in April 1969, defence priorities were turned upside down, and MOBCOM suddenly found itself equipped and structured for a role that had been dropped from first to last place. Since then, its training and equipment acquisition have been oriented toward the following tasks:

National security (and aid to civil power)

Defence of North America

NATO commitments

Peacekeeping or stability operations, and

Collateral tasks.[3]

The new priorities also signaled a move toward involving the Army more in national development projects, such as road, bridge and airfield building in remote regions and away from traditional peacetime soldiering, with its emphasis on training for war.

In future, the Army at home would spend more time working with other government departments in the development of the civil sector, and less time on the range and training field.

## THE TASKS

MOBCOM's new roles and priorities are demanding. To perform them MOBCOM's present commander, Lieutenant-General J. J. Paradis, commands forces from his headquarters at St. Hubert, P.Q., that extend from the Avalon Peninsula in Newfoundland to the Queen Charlotte Islands in the Pacific, and from the High Arctic to the Canada-United States border. The physical defence of Canada is his principal mission.

The national security function is enormous and particularly complicated — not only by distance — but by reason of the fact that MOBCOM's personnel are constantly being rotated into and out of peacekeeping missions in the Middle East and the NATO contingent in Germany.

The sovereignty protection role includes aid to civil power, which now embraces everything from supplying troops for internal security (as for example during the Quebec crisis in 1970), to fighting forest fires and guarding struck federal prisons, to civil emergency operations in times of natural disaster or nuclear attack.

In addition, the command is responsible for control of northern sovereignty and is required to maintain a continuing presence there. Since 1969 soldiers have been required to train regularly in the Arctic "which is both a practical and symbolic display of the country's sovereignty and independence."[4] The defence of North America function is really an appendage of the first priority. Under existing agreements between Canada and the United States, an attack on either country is considered an attack on both, and a joint defence would be conducted.

Next comes NATO. MOBCOM does not command the NATO force but it provides the personnel for Number 4 Canadian Mechanized Brigade Group (4 CMBG) there on a rotational basis. It has also been committed for some time to send reinforcements to Europe in an emergency.

As part of this commitment, MOBCOM maintains a quick-response airportable battalion group that is pledged for duty to NATO's northern flank to demonstrate the Alliance's solidarity in the face of political or military threats. Should reinforcement be necessary, MOBCOM is further committed to send over the CAST (Canadian Air/Sea Transportable) 6,000-man combat group. In 1971 the government increased this commitment by assigning two squadrons of CF-5 jet fighters to Allied Command Europe (ACE) for photographic reconnaissance and ground support roles on the northern flank.

The fourth priority is United Nations peacekeeping, the recognized Canadian specialty. Since 1964 MOBCOM has maintained a force of at least 500 peacekeepers in Cyprus alone, along with as many as 1,500 in the Middle East.

Finally, the so-called collateral tasks include a mixed bag of responsibilities which have grown since 1969 as part of MOBCOM's reorientation toward domestic concerns. In addition, Canada's 100-odd militia units were placed under MOBCOM's control in 1970.

## THE LEAN YEARS

Despite its increasing responsibilities, Mobile Command began to decline in strength in 1969 when the defence budget was frozen for three years. During this period, manpower dropped from 26,000 to 21,000 officers and men as part of the government's manpower reduction program. Essential stocks of ammunition and spare parts were consumed and not replaced. In 1970, the government restructured MOBCOM's fighting components from four 3,500-man combat groups to three, with headquarters in Calgary, Alberta; Petawawa, Ontario; and Valcartier, P.Q. The defunct combat group at CFB Gagetown, N.B., subsequently became the army's Combat Training Centre with a reduced complement of men.

The decision to revert to a nine-battalion, three-regiment infantry structure sowed the seeds for the eventual linguistic balkanization of the Army. In September 1969, when Leo Cadieux announced the restructuring, the government killed off five English-speaking regiments in the name of economy but retained two francophone regiments created a year earlier at Valcartier. Few soldiers were sorry to see the Canadian Guards go, but the premature death of two crack infantry regiments —the Black Watch and the Queen's Own Rifles of Canada — along with an artillery and armoured regiment, hurt morale and deprived MOBCOM of its most efficient and experienced combat units in one stroke.

New equipment was another casualty of the initial freeze period — MOBCOM could not afford to buy any. Under Hellyer's five-year plan the Army's fighting units had been equipped with 115 new CF-5 close-support jet fighters, 1,000 armoured personnel carriers (APCs) and 810 *Carl Gustav* portable anti-tank guns. Between 1968 and 1969 the artillery squadrons had received $60 million worth of the latest guns — fifty-eight air-portable 105mm Pack howitzers and fifty 155mm M109 self-propelled howitzers, similar to a tank, of which twenty were in service with the NATO brigade. But the freeze killed purchase of badly needed daily-use equipment, such as trucks (most were more than twenty years old), radio sets, combat clothing and training ammunition. And the armoured corps did not get its long promised tank.

The Centurion tank was the principal weapon of Canada's mechanized brigade group in Germany, and MOBCOM maintained about twenty of them at Gagetown to train replacement tank crews that were bound for Europe. The ancient Centurions, purchased from Britain in 1952, were scheduled to be replaced in the early 1970s under the Hellyer plan. However, they fell afoul of the 1971 White Paper, which phased the tank out of existence because "this vehicle is not compatible with Canadian-based forces."[5] Despite howls of protest, the armoured regiments in Canada and Europe were to be re-equipped for a light armour reconnaissance role, which would achieve the government's desired "compatibility of Canadian and European-based forces."[6] This decision created confusion and bitterness among the troops, and interrupted normal combined infantry-armour training in Canada. The tank decision had a greater impact on

Canada's over-all military policy in NATO and is examined in greater detail in the next chapter.

Inflation and declining manpower during the initial freeze period also led to the creeping "civilianization" of many jobs previously done by soldiers. Between 1969 and 1974, more than 1,500 base-support positions in MOBCOM were filled by lower-paid civilians as part of the government's program to trim the Command's rising personnel costs. The jobs ranged from lowly sweeper and stores clerk to electrical technician and their reallocation as civilian positions freed soldiers to return to hard pressed field units. Between 1974 and 1975 MOBCOM's military strength slipped from 19,000 to 17,500, while its civilian strength increased to 4,700 from 4,500.

Since 1969, the slow process of civilianization of support positions at military bases has eroded the Army's vital tactical reserves. To beef up its declining "sharp end," MOBCOM was forced to pull many of its base support soldiers, electricians and mechanics, for example, back into operational field units. These service corpsmen were the Army's vital "second line" reserves, ready to reinforce a battalion or regiment when needed. But civilians are not trained soldiers and cannot be used as second line troops. In a situation where MOBCOM had most of its soldiers in the field, there would be few soldiers at home to defend the proverbial store, and no more reinforcements.

In a 1976 interview, Brigadier-General George Bell (Ret'd), who was MOBCOM's deputy chief of operational requirements from 1966 to 1970, explained some of the military implications of civilianization: "We were forced into the problem of removing the separation between static base and field logistical units," which meant that "each of the major bases in the land force had a service battalion but it was both the static and field component. Today it would take a couple of bases to get a service battalion out; so that if you took a battalion and projected it operationally, the static capability of those bases would be denuded."

For MOBCOM's operational capacity, he said, "this means that the logistical units that remain, other than for those field elements that can be pulled out, there's no third or fourth line field force capable of going anywhere. For example, if you go to the workshop at Long Point (Victoria), where you've got the equivalent of the REME (Royal Canadian Electrical and Mechanical Engineers), that's all civilian people now with no commitment to move. And we don't have any field equipment to go if they were."

Trained manpower at the "sharp end" became MOBCOM's most pressing problem following the freeze period and recruitment policies did nothing to alleviate it. From 1970 to 1976 the government established more than a dozen French Language Units (FLUs) within MOBCOM to encourage francophones to make a career of the forces. To fill these new positions recruitment was slowed down in English-speaking Canada and stepped up in Quebec and other French-speaking areas of the country. But francophones failed to join in sufficient numbers to offset the steady decline in MOBCOM's over-all strength through normal attrition.

Throughout 1976 the strength of MOBCOM's sharp end declined as releases and requests for transfer from the overworked combat trades outpaced recruitment. In desperation, General Dextraze reshuffled existing positions to find another 1,500 combat troops, including the re-assignment of 300 non-combatant military personnel at NDHQ to combat units. "I must eliminate the merely desirable and keep only the essential functions fully manned," the general said. If he failed to find enough men, "then I will approach the government to advise them of our additional requirements. I am confident that they will respond favourably to my request."[7]

But the situation became worse. By January 1977, MOBCOM was 3,000 men short and General Dextraze announced a major restructuring of its resources. The eastern and western brigades would stand fast, but the airborne regiment would move from Edmonton to the Ottawa area, where it would form the heart of the new Special Service Force. "This will allow us to maintain a relatively light — airborne/airportable — quick reaction force in the demographic centre of the country in peacetime," he said, "which can be moved quickly to augment either of the flanking brigades for internal security tasks, to the Arctic, or to UN type operations."[8]

But the benefits of the restructuring were mostly cosmetic, meant as much to conceal MOBCOM's sickly condition as to make the best of a bad situation. By late 1977, when the last caisson had stopped rolling along and the dust had settled, the regrouped MOBCOM resembled an Army deployed — for the first time in Canadian history — as much along linguistic considerations as military requirements. Today Canada's army looks like this:

Army of the West: a brigade group, headquartered in Calgary, with units there and in Chilliwack and Esquimalt, B.C., Shilo and Winnipeg, Manitoba. Manpower: 4,500 (all anglophone)

Army of the East: 5e Groupement de Combat, based at Valcartier, with troops also at Gagetown and Citadel, Quebec City. Manpower: 9,000 (mainly francophone)

Army of the Centre: Based at Petawawa — about 3,500 troops — includes the Special Service Force and the 600-man 1st Battalion, Royal Canadian Regiment, in London, Ontario, tasked as Canada's quick-response battalion for NATO's northern flank. Manpower: 4,100 (bilingual mix)[9]

### "10 TAG"

MOBCOM's vital air component never really got airborne during the Trudeau years. With headquarters at St. Hubert, No. 10 Tactical Air Group (10 TAG) was formed in 1968 to provide combat and transport air support for Hellyer's globe-trotting policemen. When defence priorities changed in 1969, the group's role became less strategic and only two squadrons of CF-5 aircraft were formed instead of the four originally planned. In addition, plans to equip 10 TAG with a large variety of battle and transport helicopters were also scrapped during the freeze period because of lack of funds.

Today, the group operates all air resources engaged in close support of MOBCOM's operations. This involves fixed-wing and helicopter fire-support, reconnaissance and tactical transport over the battle area. The group is committed to provide its two CF-5 squadrons — 434 Training Squadron at Cold Lake, Alberta, and 433 Fighter Squadron at Bagotville, P.Q. — for deployment to NATO's northern flank in times of tension. Each squadron flies about a dozen operational aircraft. When Air Command was formed in 1975, the Commander of MOBCOM lost actual control of 10 TAG's resources, but he retains control while they are performing his group's primary functions.

### THE MILITIA

Since pre-Confederation the Militia had provided Canada with a large pool of citizen-soldiers who were willing to defend the nation against foe, fire and flood, and for next to nothing. They were a valuable source of semi-trained manpower to back up the Army in time of war and to help local authorities during times of civil or natural disaster. During the Cold War of the late fifties, many of the more than 60,000 active militiamen across the country were assigned a new task — aid to the civilian population in the event of nuclear attack. From Vancouver Island to Newfoundland outports the Militia drilled and trained, waiting as they always had to be called on for help.

But when Paul Hellyer took over defence in 1963, he caused an uproar among old guard Tories by slashing the Militia's strength from 60,000 to 24,000 and closing hundreds of small town defence facilities. In what would be a practice run for unification, he wanted to divert the few millions being spent to support the nation's reservoir of "Saturday night soldiers" into providing better equipment for the regular force.

The Militia was still reorganizing in 1969 when Trudeau mowed down its thinned ranks from coast to coast. In an effort to trim $15 million from defence spending, the government reduced the Militia to 20,000 men, disbanded sixty-nine units and closed forty-one armouries. When MOBCOM was assigned operational control of the Militia in 1970, it assumed a force that was broken and in decline.

The 1971 White Paper dismissed the reserves, of which the Militia made up about three quarters, as a useless contribution in the modern era where "the ratio of regulars to reserves must now be higher than at other times in our history." The paper also failed to mention a plan for general mobilization of home defence forces in the event of national emergency, during which the Militia always played a prominent role. The government's decision to let the Militia wither spurred Colonel Cecil Merritt of Vancouver to write: ". . . by the wholesale disbandment of Reserve Units, our Department of National Defence has removed (for young men and women) the opportunity for part-time service to their country. It has actually promoted in the population an indifference to the need to make individual efforts to preserve

national sovereignty. . . . Without reserves during periods of un-
rest or attack, we would be left with nothing with which our
Canadian government could exercise its sovereignty in the face of
civil panic."[10]

Major-General Bruce Legge, who retired in 1977 as senior
reserve officer in the forces, said Trudeau's reduction of the
Militia "was a terrible blow, a terrible loss. It caused a terrible loss
of identity and military presence in small towns . . . the Army lost
a reservoir of cheap local expertise in time of emergency."

It was not until 1975,when MOBCOM was desperately short of
men, that interest in the Militia was revived. Richardson suddenly
unveiled the "Total Force Concept," which called for a
rejuvenated Militia to bolster the beleaguered regular force.

But the sudden reversal in form found a Militia that was
reduced to only 13,500 men, the lowest point in its history. By
1977, despite better pay and promises of new equipment, Militia
strength had only crept up to 15,000 and was suffering a crippling
attrition rate of more than 50 percent among first-year recruits. In
1969 the Militia had 15,000 men earmarked to fill regular force
jobs in case of emergency. Today it can supply less than 3,000.

In January 1978, Danson outlined the government's latest plan
to revitalize the reserves, which he conceded had been "almost
reorganized out of existence." The reserves, and particularly the
Militia, would be beefed-up and re-equipped so they could "take
some pressure off our ground and air forces, now spread over so
many tasks that a recent study of one unit found it had barely 10
percent of its time left for training."[11] The underpinning rationale
for this ongoing Total Force approach, with a steady stream of
reserves replacing regulars for extended periods, was that Canada
would be able to meet its minimum military objectives without
having to increase the size of its permanent force above 83,000. In

a sense it is defence on the cheap, because even the best-trained reservists are not fully trained professional soldiers. Using them to plug the gaps in regular force ranks is, at best, a calculated risk.

Few Canadians realize that in 1976, when MOBCOM could no longer supply enough men on a regular basis to relieve those serving in units overseas, NDHQ began scouring Militia bases across the country for replacements. During 1977 about 330 mostly teenage militiamen served with our NATO brigade in Europe, and 217 did tours with peacekeeping forces in Cyprus and the Middle East.[12] No other NATO country permits such large numbers of semi-trained personnel to serve in these potential "hot spots."

But Danson intends to use more, and that's a major reason the government is anxious to restore the ratio of reserves to regulars that existed ten years ago, which is a repudiation of its White Paper position. "As training standards improve," said Danson, "we intend to employ more reservists on six-month tours of peacekeeping duty in Cyprus and the Middle East as well as with the Canadian Forces in Europe." To upgrade training the government has started pouring new equipment into Militia units. How bad has training been? Well, said Danson, "last spring one Militia district with four infantry units had only one mortar in working condition and no bombs for training. We can't hold reservists by telling them, as one officer did last year when he ran out of ammunition during exercises, 'point your rifles and yell bang, bang!' "[13] Now the government has embarked on a multi-million dollar program to restore old armouries and build new ones, some in the same cities and towns which were closed by Trudeau in 1969. One thing is certain: the Militia will not be revived for the $15 million the government saved by running it down.

## DOWN FOR THE COUNT

After several years of financial malnutrition and declining manpower, MOBCOM is struggling desperately to perform its assigned roles. The new priorities have had a greater impact on MOBCOM's combat capability than on any other command. Because it was the heart of Hellyer's global policekeeping force, most of its new equipment that came into service during the late sixties and early seventies was designed for that role and was incompatible with the new orientation toward internal security and national development. Jet planes and APCs were not compatible with bridge building or clearing national parks and MOBCOM got stuck with the bill. MOBCOM spent millions of dollars for equipment it could not use, and thus did not have enough left in its frozen bank account to buy what it really needed.

One glaring example of waste was the 1,000 APCs that were bought to convert the four brigades to mechanized formations in order to increase their mobility. When regiments were dropped from active service and more than 3,000 men came home from Germany, many to be released as an economy measure, hundreds of the $60,000 apiece APCs were rendered surplus to requirements. More than 200 were stored, while others decayed in under-strength regiments which could not use all they had.[14]

But the best example of waste created by the new priorities is provided by the CF-5 jet fighter aircraft, which was rendered useless even before it rolled off the assembly line at $2 million a copy. In 1966, Hellyer ordered 115 from Canadair Ltd. of Montreal for $215 million, approximately 30 percent more than it would have cost to buy direct from the patent holders, Northrup Aircraft of the United States. The twin-engine aircraft were purchased to provide ground support for peacekeepers, but the new priorities had no use for this type of plane.

The first forty-one CF-5s were delivered between 1968 and 1969, and went into service with 433 Squadron at Bagotville and 434 at Cold Lake. When defence roles were tumbled, the government admitted it did not know what to do about the remaining seventy-four aircraft, which were still to be built. Despite advice from its own air force brass and howls of protest from Opposition MPs, the government declined to cancel the contract for the remaining planes.

When the go-ahead was announced in 1970, the *Toronto Star* branded the move as "the most irresponsible waste of public funds in Canadian peacetime history."[15] Even General Frederick Sharp, the CDS, admitted he did not know what to do with the extra aircraft because financial restraints made it impossible to fly them. "We are placing more than had been originally planned in storage for financial reasons," he said, "because of the restructuring of the services we had to change our plans."[16] The government promised to find a role for the new planes, but there was one serious drawback: the CF-5 had a ferry range of just over 1,000 nautical miles and a *combat range of only 250.*

Politically, the affair did have a bright side. It was a great make-work project for Canadair and more than one critic noted that it created lots of jobs in Liberal held ridings in Quebec. Militarily, however, the seventy-four extra aircraft cost MOBCOM $138 million during the freeze period, which wiped out any hope it had to purchase more useful equipment. In 1971, the last few CF-5s rolled from the assembly line into storage at North Bay and Trenton, where about twenty still slumber in heavy plastic sheets.

Roles for a handful of the CF-5s were finally spelled out in the 1971 White Paper. The two existing squadrons were earmarked for duty on NATO's northern flank in times of tension or war. Otherwise, they would be employed in Canada as training aircraft and for "quick reaction photographic reconnaissance," whatever that was. However, the CF-5 is woefully inadequate for either role, as military critics pointed out.

"It would fall mercifully into the sea before it got a hundred miles off Newfoundland," said Air Vice-Marshal Robert Cameron, who, along with other military men, was aghast at the prospect of using the CF-5 in Europe. "The government had to find *some* use for the blessed things, so Macdonald came up with the NATO thing... which is nonsense," he said. With a maximum combat range of 250 miles, the CF-5 would face serious survival problems if it ever found itself in combat. In case it was chased from its immediate combat zone, or if its home field was destroyed, "that would be the end of the plane and the pilot," said Cameron. "For a combat plane," he added, "it's too bloody slow."* To get the planes to Europe the government had to rig two Boeing 707 jet transports for mid-air refuelling; it takes two days to ferry one squadron of CF-5s to the northern flank area.

Major George Lowes, a career air force officer and author of articles on military aviation in Canada, said the "CF is no good for the Canadian role in Europe. It's ideal for teaching people how to fly, but it doesn't have the time-over-point-to-loiter capability ideally suited for Europe ... it's no good for us, here or there. It's a white elephant, an expensive white elephant and we never should have bought it."

STUCK FOR TRUCKS

Budget restraints during the initial freeze period gave MOBCOM's rolling stock a flat tire, delaying for several years the

---

*Top speed is 1,000 mph compared to 1,500-plus for conventional Soviet fighters.

arrival of thousands of badly needed trucks. For example, on March 30, 1967, Hellyer approved the purchase of 3,203 one-and-a-quarter-ton utility trucks to replace the Army's fading workhorse fleet of three-quarter-ton trucks, which were bought in 1952. The new Chrysler built vehicles would cost $48.3 million and were intended to arrive in service between 1970 and 1972. They were "urgently" needed, said CDS General Jean Allard in a 1967 memo, because the old ones "are becoming extremely difficult and expensive to maintain and as a result they are reducing the operational effectiveness of the field units to which they are issued."[17] The order was cancelled in 1970, along with plans to purchase new jeeps and two-and-a-half and five-ton trucks, because MOBCOM's budget no longer had money to pay for them.

MOBCOM's surface mobility suffered badly as a result of the delay and in some cases training exercises ground to a halt altogether as veteran trucks simply caved in. In 1974, in a belated effort to get the Army rolling again, the government launched a frantic buying program to replace 8,400 units of the forces entire fleet of 10,000 trucks, most of which were earmarked for MOBCOM. How bad were the trucks? "A civilian firm would have gone bankrupt long ago in terms of vehicle maintenance," said a veteran Army mechanic. "It must be costing the government a fortune" to keep these trucks rolling.[18]

Training also suffered. In October 1974, an annual full-scale training exercise involving the 2nd Battalion, Royal Canadian Regiment, was stalled for twenty-four hours south of Fredericton, N.B., because their ancient "four-wheel drive battle vehicles couldn't hold the road. . . . Whatever else the October exercise to Camp Aldershot showed, it demonstrated that the basic equipment now being used by what is supposed to be Canada's ready response defence force is not up to the needs of operational efficiency even on the highways of Canada."[19] Some of the 8,400 new trucks are now in service and the remainder are scheduled to roll in by 1982. The cost: $120 million, about $70 million more than originally projected before procurement plans were scrapped.[20]

### FIRING BLANKS

The financial drain on MOBCOM's budget for hardware it could not use severely degraded the level of combat training, and thus of readiness, throughout the command as stocks of ammunition and tools were purposely run down to save for other requirements. [21] Ammunition levels climbed slightly in 1974, when the post-freeze budget provided for a small increase in ammunition spending, but "expenditures were cut to the bone" the following year as double-digit inflation forced further economies. Combat training was all but suspended in Canada, where units cancelled routine practice shoots to provide ammunition for their colleagues serving with the NATO brigade in Germany. On October 17, 1975, James Richardson told Army officials they would have to "live within the budget" when they pleaded for more ammunition.[22]

As late as 1976, the CDA singled out lack of training ammunition as a major cause of the high attrition rate in the combat trades. Men join the sharp end of the army because they want "action," which involves expending sufficient amounts of ammunition in field training to remain "sharp." When ammunition started to dry up in the early seventies, men began leaving the combat trades. The CDA pointed this out in a resolution to the government: "The current inability to provide minimum quantities of ammunition required has resulted in a reduction of standards," and urged the government to procure enough ammunition "to ensure the maintenance of training standards and to maintain interest levels essential to recruiting and retention of personnel."[23] How bad was the shortage?

In January 1976, Major-General George Kitching, former Commander of the Army's Central Command, told of his recent visit to an infantry battalion in Calgary: "When you talk to a crew of a 106 recoilless (rifle) — and they had *one* out there, there was a sergeant and four men — the sergeant had fired a total of twenty-two rounds, because he had been on a course in the States when he had fired most of those rounds. The rest of the crew were down to two and three rounds, over as many years. What is the point of trying to fool those soldiers? Of course they will leave, who the hell wouldn't?"[24]

The situation was even worse in the armoured corps. "There is such a shortage of artillery, tank and mortar ammunition that virtually none will be fired this year or next," reported the Royal Canadian Armoured Corps Association, in October 1975. A typical training situation for an armoured squadron, one senior officer said, "is to have three or four shells to fire and to schedule courses simultaneously for everyone connected with a tank to optimize the use of ammunition. That's economically sound on paper but militarily absurd."[25] Even the Combat Arms School at Gagetown, where tankmen learn their trade, was suffering: "Ammunition restrictions are easing so courses are getting a few more rounds. But no gun camps are scheduled for Canadian based regiments in Gagetown during 1976" because of the Olympics.[26]

Artillery regiments were pleased to possess the highly rated multi-purpose 105mm Pack howitzer, but unhappy because they could not fire them. In 1977 an artillery captain from Shilo, Manitoba, said his unit had eight guns but for three years it had been down to 500 rounds a year for the entire unit. "That works out to 62.5 rounds of ammo per gun," he quipped, "hardly enough to get the barrels warm or keep the crew sighted in."

The policy to deliberately deplete ammunition levels and spares had other serious effects. General Bell explained: "It raised the inevitable cost for the force at any future time we tried to re-equip it. It produced a condition where we ate up what reserves we had . . . in ammunition and defence stores and other things, which were not replaced. And I'd say that we are very hard pressed to meet our basic operational stocks in-country to support the thirty-day, ninety-day backup in Europe.

"At the same time, the lack of money to go into purchasing ammunition or into development of new technology meant that the infrastructure that we had for producing this went under. In other words, we were producing 20-pounder ammunition for the Centurion tank; we were producing 76mm ammunition for the FN rifle; we were producing special explosives at Valcartier. Go to Valcartier today and they're only producing one thing, and that's a tungsten carbide core bullet for the machine gun.

"A lot of that technology, a lot of the capacity for research has gone because of the starvation of defence. And the result was: if you don't have it (shells) in stock, you don't have it in sufficient numbers to deploy it in sufficient numbers, so the man going through his training is not getting enough training, and annual practice camps, and that has become increasingly a problem. That is being resolved a little now as the money's being put back into the system, but it's too late . . . it won't restore any of the industries who went under."

### TANKS
The decision to scrap the tank and convert armoured regiments to a light armour reconnaissance role created serious training

problems for the Army's entire combat team. Old fashioned as it may seem, the tank is still the steely heart of land combat operations, providing fire support and protection for infantry. When the Centurions were mothballed in 1972, the reality went out of combined training exercises. "Trucks would double as tanks," said an infantry colonel, "and the men would run along behind them shouting, 'get down you fools, this is a tank!' It was all rather bizarre and pointless."[27]

With the tanks gone, armoured regiments waited patiently for the direct fire-support vehicle promised in the White Paper, but it did not appear. Neither did the long-overdue armoured vehicle to replace the 120 twenty-year-old Ferret scout cars that had become the Army's major piece of fighting armour. Finally, in October 1976, Canada announced it would buy 128 Leopard C-1 tanks from Germany, most of which would go to the NATO brigade. But lack of heavy armour — or *any* armour to be exact — had severely degraded combat training in Canada, as Danson explained in 1977: "Officials say the tactical integrity of the Army's all-arm combat team had deteriorated since 1969, when tanks were withdrawn from most army bases in Canada.

"Combat elements equipped with the incompatible mix could not keep pace with each other in cross-country operations, assaulting water obstacles or in training at the formation level.

"Also affected was the ability to train augmentees for Canada's armoured element on NATO duty in Europe."[28]

In February 1977, Danson announced the purchase of 350 Swiss-made Piranha armoured cars to replace the Ferrets, which had been phased out of service years earlier by the British. A search for a new WARV (wheeled armoured reconnaissance vehicle) started in 1970 but was stalled by financial restraints. Revived in 1972, the project was shelved until 1974, following the decision not to replace the Centurion with the British Scorpion mini-tank. This left armoured regiments to operate with Ferrets and a handful of Lynx tracked vehicles, which were jury-rigged APCs hastily converted to a reconnaissance role in the absence of proper equipment.

In mid-1974, DND launched a controversial project to find a single multi-purpose armoured vehicle that could replace the Ferret, Lynx and defunct Scorpion. Despite military objections to the plan, a team from DND and Supply and Services examined fourteen possible contenders before narrowing the field down to three : Piranha, the American Commando and the Brazilian Urutu. The winner of tough winter trails at Wainwright, Alberta, would become the Army's new three-in-one AVGP (armoured vehicle general purpose).

The forces planned to buy 715 AVGPs in three models for a price of about $200 million, according to the actual Treasury Board approval.[29] They would be used as "a family of wheeled, armoured vehicles . . . to perform operational tasks in the defence of North America, maintaining Canadian sovereignty, internal security operations and peacekeeping operations."[30] Piranha emerged as DND's pick in mid-1975, but its procurement was held up for two years because of an inter-departmental dispute, during which time the price doubled.

In 1975, DND's submission on Piranha to Treasury Board was blocked by officials of the trade department's Latin American division, who favoured purchase of the Brazilian Urutu as a means of increasing trade with the South American country. "Board officials . . . held it up," said a defence spokesman, "suggesting that more study and consideration be given to the Urutu."[31] Piranha had nosed the Urutu out during winter trials, which proved too much for a vehicle designed for use in an equatorial climate.

Finally in January 1977, Treasury Board agreed to the Piranha deal. In the meantime, however, the cost of the vehicle had almost doubled and DND could only afford to buy 350 at a price of $174 million. "We didn't get what we wanted . . . 350 is only half of the total required," said a DND source. "We barely have enough to bring the Canadian regiments up to near strength; there's nothing left over . . . for Europe, and there's no guarantee any more will ever be ordered." Over-all plans call for a total production of 700 vehicles, but military officials doubt more will ever be purchased. The vehicle itself is an amalgam of other machines, all tacked together to satisfy Canada's requirement for three different models in one. The six-wheel Piranhas will roll into service in Canada between October 1978 and early 1981 in three forms.

There will be 152 "Cougar" fire-support vehicles, carrying Scorpion turrets with a 76mm gun. Canada rejected the heavier *tracked* Scorpion as a replacement for the tank, but will use its fighting top half on a wheeled vehicle with considerably less broken-field capability, which is an essential requirement for a fire-support machine. Assigned to protect forward scout vehicles, acquisition of a wheeled model presumes that reconnaissance and fighting would be confined to paved roads.

Another 179 will come as the "Grizzly" armoured personnel carrier, designed to carry nine combat-equipped troops and armed with an obsolete 50mm machine gun. Nineteen will be "Husky" maintenance and recovery vehicles, equipped to tow other vehicles away during combat. They are not armed.

What is puzzling to defence watchers is the distribution of the Piranhas. Regular force units in Canada will receive only 197 of the total order, not enough to replace already exhausted stocks of Ferrets and Lynx. Militia units will get 114 new vehicles. In the case of the Grizzly, units in Canada are still bursting at the seams with the APCs purchased by Hellyer. The Cougar is more sophisticated and has greater firepower than the old APC, but it is not going to the NATO brigade in Germany, which has a greater need for it. Neither are the nineteen Husky recovery vehicles, yet planners admit they cannot find a useful role for them at home.

There is, however, another reason why the APCs were kept in Canada which defence officials do not like to talk about — that Ottawa bought them to deal with possible armed insurrection over Quebec separation. In 1977 Tory MP Michael Forrestall said "inside information is that 25 percent of them (APCs) are earmarked for the use of civil authorities with military drivers." The Piranha is one of the most effective anti-riot vehicles ever made, and it is used for such purposes by police in West Germany and South America. "Trudeau doesn't want to be caught as he was in the 1970 crisis," added Forrestall, "without such a top-notch anti-riot vehicle."[32] Danson has denied the allegation yet the strange dispersal of Piranhas close to the Quebec border has left many people wondering.

### A SPLIT PERSONALITY

When the government killed the five English-speaking regiments in order to make way for new francophone units, it created a linguistic split in MOBCOM which is still growing. "If anything damaged the Army," said AVM Cameron, "it was the killing off of the famous English regiments. . . . It split the ranks down the middle, very neatly, and stirred up all sorts of racial antagonism that never existed before." The passing of the celebrated Black Watch provides a good example of how morale and efficiency were sacrificed to the cause of bilingualism.

For decades the Watch was one of the most efficient and popular regiments in the country. It "had the highest re-enlistment rate of any English-language regiment in Canada because it had an excellent spirit built on a great tradition," said its Colonel-in-

Chief, J. G. Bourne.[33] The Watch boasted more battle honours and Victoria Crosses than any other Canadian unit and was repeatedly rated the best infantry regiment in the nation.

In 1969 it won the Hamilton Gault Trophy for achieving the highest proficiency for rifle marksmanship in the Canadian Army.[34] And at NATO talks in Paris, the Watch's 2nd battalion was praised for being the best unit in a multi-national exercise on the northern flank, the area Canada was committed to defend in the event of war.[35] For many who lamented the death of the Watch, it was hard to believe Leo Cadieux's words that it was being done "on the seniority principle,"[36] while the two recently created francophone regiments were retained. They were the 12e Régiment blinde du Canada (armoured) and the 5e Régiment d'artillerie légère du Canada, formed at Valcartier in 1968.

When the Watch was disbanded, some of its men were absorbed into the Royal Canadian Regiment; others retired rather than suffer the trauma of rebadging. At the final parade, when the Watch's colours and battle honours were laid to rest, dozens of officers wore black arm bands as a symbol of their grief. "The troops accepted the news with grace and deep hurt," said Lieutenant-Colonel "Scotty" Morrison, commanding officer of the first battalion, "like a family that suffered a tragic loss of kinfolk."[37] Years later, defence analyst Professor Duncan Fraser wrote: "A young private soldier in the Black Watch wrote to me of his heartbreak at seeing his regimental home destroyed. It means a great deal to the soldier, this regimental home. Soldiers after all don't get very much, but an awful lot is asked of them."[38]

Death of the Watch also fanned Gaelic tempers across the Maritimes, which regarded the regiment as its own. One St. John man sent a parcel to Trudeau containing a Black Watch kilt and sporran; the sporran bore the regiment's motto, *nemo me impune lacessit* — No one insults me with impunity. Even the usually do-cile *Halifax Chronicle-Herald* reminded Ottawa that the Watch was the last and the greatest of the Highland regiments, and was thus a sacred trust as well as a symbol of the "Scottish fact" in Canada. It was also the last infantry regiment in the Maritimes and more than 90 percent of its men were maritimers. Despite appeals to save it, the Black Watch died on July 1, 1970.

Morale is a difficult quality to measure, but there is no doubt it has a direct bearing on a regiment's efficiency. A happy regiment is an efficient regiment; an unhappy one is not. During wartime a regiment's morale is maintained by a curious mixture of blood, loyalty, tradition and a tenacious will to survive. But in the monotonous drone of peacetime soldiering, a diferent mixture is required to keep spirits high. Such a mix is provided by the twin pillars of morale: love for the regimental home and a fair prospect for promotion. Remove them and morale and efficiency topple, as they did when the English regiments died.

While promotion opportunities in other English-speaking regiments declined due to the influx of rebadged personnel, they increased sharply in new FLUs which naturally lacked trained francophones at senior levels. A new FLU meant more promotions for French-Canadians and a longer wait on the roster for anglophones. To many the "revenge of the cradle" had arrived, as the armoured corps discovered in 1971.

#### RANK PROBLEMS

The "corporals' mess" blew up in February 1971, when the Calgary-based Lord Strathcona Horse armoured regiment was told in a secret message from NDHQ that corporals could not expect to be promoted to sergeant for at least two years unless they were willing to learn French and serve at Valcartier. Despite government denials, the affair confirmed the worst fears of anglophone soldiers that FLUs would cost them promotions.

The message, dated January 21, said that sergeants were desperately needed for the newly created 12e Blinde regiment, but they had to speak French or be willing to learn. The situation was a direct result of disbanding the Fort Garry Horse and distributing many of its NCOs to the Strathconas. This created "a surplus of sergeants (anglophone) in armoured corps units," noted a confidential report, which revealed that the two English-speaking armoured regiments in Canada were thirty-six sergeants above requirement, while the 12e Blinde was twenty-eight short.[39] The situation for corporals was much worse. The two anglophone regiments had a battalion of corporals — 328 — but required only 84, a situation which killed any hope of promotion.[40]

Throughout 1970, DND ran a high-powered recruiting campaign in Quebec to obtain enough francophones to bring the lower levels of the 12e blinde up to strength. When it failed, the department appealed to the very men whose regiment it had destroyed a year earlier. "In order to improve this unsatisfactory situation," reported a confidential ministerial inquiry, "and having exhausted the supply of eligible French-speaking candidates for senior NCO training, it was reluctantly decided to make an effort to fill the shortages with unilingual English NCOs (sergeants) who were willing to learn French and serve with the 12th Armoured Regiment. In September 1970, a request for volunteers was made to each English-speaking armoured regiment with no success."[41] Attention then turned to corporals.

In February 1971, Donald Macdonald explained that in order to bring the 12e blinde up to strength, "we first loaded the qualifying training course with all eligible French-speaking corporals who placed sufficiently high on the merit list. We then offered the top twenty-five English-speaking corporals on the merit list an opportunity to take trades training and language training.[42] DND sources, however, say that many francophone privates were promoted to corporal in order to get them on the merit list, from where they could be slipped into the next NCO training course and promoted to sergeant.

Finally, the government admitted that six English-speaking corporals who had initially been selected to take the course had been kicked off for refusing to belatedly "volunteer" to serve with the 12e blinde. It was explained they were only being "deferred" for one course because of the emergency, but a confidential memo suggests that was not the case. "They will be given training *provided* they maintain their position on the merit list, but their promotion will depend on vacancies." In short, they would regain their earned positions in the promotion stream if and when the need for francophone personnel had been satisfied. It is still not satisfied.

The "corporals' mess" was not confined to armoured regiments; it affected infantry and artillery units the same way. The incident provoked angry debate in regimental messes across the country. One of the Strathcona corporals bumped from the NCO course filed a redress of grievance to the minister, but it was quashed to cool down the anger brewing in anglophone regiments. To soothe ruffled anglophone soldiers, the forces' information directorate quickly dispatched a slick press release to military newspapers which explained that the 12e Blinde phenomenon "was strictly a manning problem" and would not happen again. It mildly chastised the six reluctant anglophone corporals for not volunteering to serve at Valcartier, which would have assured them promotion. "It won't have any effect on normal promotions in English-speaking regiments," the release said, but "what it did was provide anyone interested in learning French and serving with a French regiment the opportunity for an accelerated promotion."[43]

But the situation did happen again in MOBCOM many times and the gulf between English- and French-speaking soldiers widened. "These accelerated promotions cause lots of problems," said Major Lowes. "Even if they say you'll be considered on the next promotion board, how do you know there's going to be another promotion board? There's been a hell of a lot of good infantry people, your *line* people, have got out over this."

This practice was confirmed by a former Army Captain, who retired in 1976 after twenty-five years' service. Born in Quebec of English-speaking parents, and fluently bilingual, he was commissioned from the ranks in 1970 and returned to Valcartier. He was a military policeman. "In 1972 the security people at NDHQ were having trouble finding five francophone NCOs to promote to Chief Warrant Officer.* I asked if they had to be bilingual and the answer was 'no, they have to be French.' Five were finally selected after a long search but we had to go farther than thirty names down the merit list to find five francophones who had even the basic promotion requirement. They were promoted . . . it caused an awful stink."

Because of the accelerated promotions many men left the Army, the majority from English-speaking combat units where opportunities for advancement were almost nil. To compensate for the steady drain in trained sharp end personnel, NDHQ launched a program "to reduce the rate of attrition on the combat trades, and to increase the number of trade options available to the career-minded soldier. Started in October 1976, the Land Operations Trade Reassignment Program (LOTRP) gave a

*The highest NCO rank.

combat soldier an opportunity to remuster to a noncombatant trade without having to quit the Army altogether. The program met with little success because most soldiers knew there are few openings in the "blunt end" trades.[44] The steady outflow of new blood is the Army's major manpower problem, but loss of too much old blood has caused problems of its own.

In January 1976, Major-General Bruce Macdonald (Retired), former Deputy Chief of Personnel, told delegates to the CDA in Ottawa: "It's criminal that we should permit the level of professionalism in the combat elements of our forces to decline in the way they have, because in the ultimate analysis, if we get into trouble, we can recruit from civilian life . . . but you cannot find anywhere the men to train soldiers and lead them into combat.

"My concern is that we are in grave danger of losing the techniques for training and fighting, which we bought and paid for with the blood of your comrades and mine. This is a national disgrace, and the time is not here, the time is long past when we should stand up and say, to whoever has ears to listen, in the name of God, look at the world that surrounds us, and if you think it's getting more stable, then you're not reading the same papers as I am."

### DEFENCELESS

The forces of Mobile Command are not capable of defending any part of Canada without the help of American allies, which is in a sense an abdication of the very sovereignty the new defence priorities sought to secure. This is the verdict of most generals, who point out that a sharp end force of less than 10,000 men is too light in substance to defend a country of three-and-a-half million square miles.

In 1975, the Royal Canadian Artillery Association wrote:

"Ground combat forces stand as the ultimate guarantee of our nation's sovereignty and, indeed, of our national integrity: to honour our international commitments, to guarantee the life and property of our citizens, to ensure that public order is maintained, and to safeguard the liberties inherent in our democratic process. In 1968 we had 22,000 trained combat soldiers; today we have 10,000 . . . our combat capability has declined by more than 50 percent. We have too much tail and too few teeth."[45]

On paper MOBCOM has 17,500 personnel, yet only 9,901 are filling combat positions; the rest are support personnel of one sort or another. With this handful of troops MOBCOM is supposed to defend the physical territory of Canada and to provide a variety of assistance to civilian authorities in peace and in war. "I don't know who they (Government) think they are fooling;" said R.S. Malone, "but the Army today can't field a properly equipped brigade at either end of the country without robbing people from the centre." Even then, most of the combat equipment is too light or too old to be much good.

It appears impossible to separate defence of Canada and defence of North America because "in the event of a requirement to defend the land mass of North America," the White Paper points out, "a mutual support arrangement exists with the United States." In such event, the ALCANUS agreement would come into operation. This provides for American forces to operate under Canadian command if the area of operations was within Canadian territory and vice versa. But the type and size of forces Canada could contribute are woefully inadequate.

The new two and a half brigade structure of MOBCOM leaves Western Canada almost devoid of combat troops and modern equipment. From headquarters at Calgary, Brigadier-General Patrick Mitchell commands a force similar to an old fashioned brigade group — three infantry battalions, a field artillery regiment, an armoured reconnaissance regiment, a tactical helicopter squadron and an overstretched signals regiment. The 4,500 officers and men in the command are scattered from Vancouver Island to northern Alberta, and only about half of them are combat troops. In 1977, when the airborne regiment was moved to Ottawa, the Command lost much of its ability to work in northern Canada. This "Army of the West" is responsible for defending that part of Canada that runs westward from the Lakehead (northern Ontario) to the Queen Charlotte Islands, from the High Arctic to the U.S. border. Superimposed on a map of Europe, this area would cover most of the continent, from Arctic Russia to Britain. Aside from the enormity of the area, there are other problems.

Tactical helicopter support for ground troops located in Esquimalt and Calgary is based at Namao, Alberta, near Edmonton. Home defence plans call for manning of strategic strongholds in mountainous areas. However, protests from the Indian Affairs Department have for several years halted training in the "national park areas in the mountains where one would expect the Army of the West to be most proficiently capable."[46]

In terms of equipment, the western brigade is not healthy. Until recently its trucks were the oldest in the Army, despite the requirement to work in mountains and sub-zero temperatures. The infantry battalions are short one company, operating with 600 men instead of 850, like most battalions throughout MOBCOM. They are reasonably equipped with light weapons, but the artillery lacks modern medium guns that give it real flexibility. The armoured regiment has no tanks and only a handful of armoured cars. The only main battle tanks in the area are German and British units training at Shilo, Manitoba, and Suffield, Alberta. They are not available for Canadian use.

In the east, the "Army of Quebec" — 5e brigade — embraces all land forces in *la belle province* and more than 2,000 men at the Combat Training Centre in Gagetown. Most of the brigade's units are FLUs located in Quebec City or at Valcartier, site of its headquarters, fourteen miles away.

The brigade is responsible for the physical defence of Eastern Canada, from the Ontario-Quebec border to Newfoundland, and for specific regional responsibilities in the province of Quebec.[47] Although better equipped than most parts of MOBCOM, the brigade has trouble keeping its francophone personnel, possibly the busiest group of soldiers in Canada.

One infantry battalion of the *Van Doos* is stationed permanently in Germany to maintain the "French fact" in Canada's NATO contingent. To man it, personnel from the other two battalions are constantly rotated back and forth from Quebec on a man-for-man basis. Since each soldier posted to Germany takes thirty days leave prior to going, and vice versa, there is a constant drain upon the two battalions in Canada which are at present under strength by 250 to 300 men. In reality, all of the brigade's FLUs are undermanned and have trouble keeping their younger men, despite several years of accelerated promotions and envied proximity to big city life in Quebec and Montreal.

In terms of equipment, the brigade is better off than the western brigade. The Combat Training Centre at Gagetown recently shed its two dozen old Centurion tanks for new Leopards. Tactical air support is supplied by one squadron of CF-5 fighters and helicopters at Bagotville; but the bulk of tactical transport helicopters is located 1,000 miles away, at Gagetown. In short, 5e brigade is too thin on the ground and in the air to cover a significant area of eastern Canada in either peacetime or war.

In the centre, Ontario, the newly created Special Service Force is apparently ready to defend central Canada and the government in Ottawa, as well as provide airborne troops for overseas. In reality, the new centre force is an undermanned, undergunned skeleton in armour, tricked out with a fancy name. Its creation was due more to shrinking resources than sensible military planning and General Dextraze's statement that it "must be capable . . . using reservists, of expanding to full airborne regiment *plus* a brigade in time of emergency/mobilization,"[48] is ludicrous. Canada has fewer than 3,000 militiamen who can be effectively mobilized and General Dextraze has admitted privately there is no mobilization plan.

The bulk of the centre force is based at CFB Petawawa, 110 miles northwest of Ottawa. Its sharp end there consists of 3,500 men — one under-strength and ill-equipped battalion of infantry, armour and artillery — and supporting logistic units. A second infantry battalion, 1st RCR at London, Ontario, the newly designated quick response force for NATO's northern flank, has no air transport closer than Trenton, excluding commercial jet, in case it is needed. And when the crack airborne regiment arrived at Petawawa last summer, it was on a wave of speculation that it was moving close to Quebec in case of trouble with the separatist government of René Lévesque.

**HELPING OUT AT HOME**

Mobile Command is the primary source of manpower, equipment, training and experience for internal security tasks, says a government report, which comprises "internal security (or aid to the civil power), civil emergency operations (peace and war) and control and surveillance operations in Canada."[49] The list of responsibilities is endless, but the resources to cope with them are not. "The Army has pretty well lost the capability to defend anything in the country," said General George Bell. "The civil power role? It can't do it properly without more men and equipment."

The most visible use of the military to maintain internal law and order occurred during the Quebec crisis of 1970, when 10,000 troops guarded government officials and buildings in Ottawa and Quebec province. Since then MOBCOM has supplied troops to guard several federal prisons when the guards walked out, for Olympic security, and for policing disaster areas. But the Army is becoming less and less capable of performing these roles as manpower continues to drop.

During the 1976 Summer Olympic Games in Montreal, for example, MOBCOM supplied most of the 16,000 regular troops assigned to provide security and a host of other services. To meet this obligation, Lieutenant-General Jacques Chouinard cancelled all summer leaves and training courses, denuded his regular and reserve units, and ran the operation from his headquarters at St. Hubert. "The Olympics showed the state we are now in," said General Bell. "If two emergencies were going on at opposite ends of the country, Mobile Command would have to choose which one to attend and which one to overlook."

MOBCOM has the responsibility to protect and care for the civilian population in the event of nuclear attack or other major disaster,[50] yet civil defence was ignored in the 1971 White Paper. This is surprising because a nuclear strike against the United States is admitted to be a possibility, with the consequent involvement of Canada in the role of passive victim.[51] How MOBCOM would tend to the care and feeding of victims in, say, southern Ontario after a nuclear attack against Detroit, is not known. The Army and Militia have no vehicles that can operate in a contaminated environment and only a handful of regular soldiers are equipped with suitable protective clothing. "The fact is," noted John Gellner, "that they (soldiers and citizens alike) are not protected and will not be if the government continues to pay as little attention to civil defence as it has, up to now."[52]

In 1972, one expert wrote: "Our present regular forces, by reason of their small numbers and despite their high standards of training, could neither stop the bomb nor keep civil order in our large territory under the shock of nuclear attack."[53]

Hypothetically, in the event of nuclear attack, the Army would work in close cooperation with the Civil Emergency Measures Program, which has been funded by DND for several years. In 1974, however, as part of James Richardson's austerity drive to find more money for capital expenditure, the program's annual operating grant of $3 million was cut in half. Since then the program has absorbed less than a fifth of one percent of the total defence budget.[54]

In addition, the rundown condition of the Militia has robbed the regular Army — and the country — of the primary source of semi-trained people to cope with internal emergencies. There is no known mobilization plan, and even if there were, "we might be able to muster up 3,000 all ranks (officers and men) who could be fitted into the regular forces," said a militia brigadier.[55] Most militia units are totally devoid of mobile artillery and few have enough rifles to arm thirty men. Few units have protective clothing for a nuclear environment, yet their drill halls are designated as post-nuclear strike aid stations. As a source of strength to the public in times of civil strife or national defence, "the Militia would be hard pressed to defend even their own drill halls."[56]

### SLOWBOAT TO NATO

MOBCOM's eastern brigades, along with American and British allies, are responsible for the defence of NATO's northern flank, but it is doubtful the Canadians could get there in time to make a meaningful contribution. If they did arrive in time, they would probably find themselves without vital air support and stranded with no way to get out.

The first commitment involves being ready to deploy either or both of an airportable infantry battalion of 700 men and a squadron of CF-5 fighters. This would be handled by the 1st Battalion, RCR at London, and 433 Squadron at Cold Lake. On paper the concept looks fine, but the thought of its actual execution has worried military planners since the politicians made the commitment in the early seventies.

In the first case, it is doubtful the 700-man battalion could arrive in Denmark or Norway in less than four or five days — not the few hours considered essential to a successful defence. In 1976, NATO Assistant Secretary-General Colin Humphrey urged Canada to find ways to ensure that its troops could get to Europe faster in the event of an East-West conflict. The deteriorating condition of Canada's military airlift capacity was well known to NATO planners, who stressed that reinforcements would have to arrive in hours, not days, if they were to have a chance of stopping the Russians from reaching the Rhine.[57] The recent shuffle of MOBCOM's components has not helped the situation, nor has the designation of 1 RCR as its quick-response battalion.

As an infantry battalion, 1 RCR has limited "jump" capability and its men could only be delivered to the flank area if airfields there were still intact and in friendly hands. The battalion could be flown to the flank in two or three days if the forces' five Boeing 707s could be grouped together quickly at London, which is unlikely. Its equipment, however, would travel by slower Hercules and thus arrive much later — if the lumbering, unarmed "Hercs" could get through at all. If the 707s managed to get the troops to the flank on time, this would delay the timely arrival of vital fighter cover because the 707s are not designed to carry troops and fuel CF-5s at the same time. In such event, troops could be without air support or major pieces of combat equipment, such as artillery and APCs, for at least two days after arriving in the combat zone. Finally, 1 RCR is not as yet equipped with a full range of portable anti-tank weapons, a critical requirement in a combat theatre involving heavily armoured Soviet forces, although steps are being taken to remedy the situation. "We could not get them over in time to be effective," said General Bell, "nor is there any machinery to get them out."

Should reinforcements be necessary (and they will be) the CAST commitment comes into play, in which MOBCOM's eastern brigades would send over a 6,000-man combat group. The CAST commitment, although politically appeasing to European allies, is militarily impractical for several reasons. Richardson, in his memo to Cabinet, urged the government to withdraw the troop offer because Canadian soldiers could find themselves in a death trap on the northern flank.

"There are real problems of a practical nature associated with the CAST commitment," he said. "In the first place, the planned deployment area in Denmark is an extension of the North German Plain where hostilities would almost inevitably involve heavy armoured combat (tanks) for which the combat group is not equipped. It would therefore be dependent upon armoured support from adjacent allied forces, which in fact have insufficient armour to meet adequately their own requirements and *thus no surplus to provide the necessary support to make the Canadian formulation viable in combat* . . . On military grounds, therefore, consideration should be given to negotiating out of the Danish dimension of the CAST commitment."

Richardson continued: "The military practicality of the entire CAST concept is open to question because of problems associated with the sealift aspect. It is rather doubtful whether adequate shipping capacity (which Norway is committed to provide) would in fact be available *to carry out the movement in time for the force to be useful.* Further, the ships in question would be highly vulnerable to enemy attack, and to have any reasonable prospect of getting through would require powerful protection against submarines, surface and air attack en route. *In all probability Canada would have to provide that protection from its own resources. Even on the assumption that Canada will maintain maritime and air forces with the combat capabilities required, it is doubtful whether, in the situation envisaged, they could be made available in adequate numbers."*

Before resigning, Richardson pushed hard to get Cabinet to choose one of the three options outlined in his memo. The first would limit the CAST force to Norway, "for which our forces are suited;" the others included reducing it to "a reinforced airportable battalion group of possibly 1,500 men," or "getting out of it completely." If the latter course was adopted, it "would probably require that Canada offer an increase in its NATO contribution elsewhere."

In the last analysis should CAST be deployed in Europe in sufficient time to be of strategic value, Mobile Command would be so utterly drained of military manpower that it could neither reinforce its men abroad nor defend its own bases at home.

PEACEKEEPING

Although Trudeau dropped peacekeeping to the bottom of the priority list, it is still MOBCOM's biggest chore, and the heaviest drain on its manpower.

"We have 1,100 troops over in the Middle East," said General Chouinard in 1977. "If only we had them in Canada, what a difference it would make."[58] He also has 500 troops in Cyprus, where they form a thin green line of sanity between warring

Greek-Cypriot and Turkish-Cypriot factions. In 1969, when peacekeeping was downgraded, Canada had fewer than 900 peacekeepers abroad.*

With steadily declining manpower, the constant rotation of trained soldiers between Europe and peacekeeping missions puts an enormous strain on MOBCOM's resources. The constant moving around is an adventure for the single soldier, but it often creates hardships for the married man who must leave his family behind. This continual uprooting is considered a major cause of the soaring release rate among career soldiers, who are the backbone of a peacetime force. MOBCOM is rapidly approaching the point where it will no longer be able to answer the UN's calls for help.

Today the Command maintains about 1,500 regular soldiers abroad; the remaining 200-odd are drawn mainly from the Militia. On the surface the requirement would not appear to pose serious problems for a force of more than ten times that number, but it does. For the most part, peacekeepers are not ordinary troops; they are trade specialists whose skills are needed as much at home as they are abroad. Peacekeeping assignments siphon off the cream of Canada's soldiers. Richardson, in his memo, explained why MOBCOM needs more men to cope even with limited peacekeeping operations:

> Experience in the past has shown that in most instances, both for political and technical reasons, requests to Canada have been for contingents of support and service personnel for logistics, communications, transport and related purposes rather than for formed operational units such as infantry and reconnaissance units. Although peacekeeping was not singled out as a special issue in the

*Canada's peacekeepers work under seven UN mandates: five are associated with Cyprus and the Middle East; the others involved small observer missions in Pakistan and Korea.

Phase 1 memorandum, the continuing requirement, in a peacekeeping operation such as UNEF/UNDOF* to provide substantial numbers of personnel, and particularly skilled support and service personnel, places a burden on the Canadian Armed forces, which in the light of reductions in total regular force strength in recent years, has become increasingly onerous.

To meet current and foreseeable peacekeeping requirements, there might usefully be earmarked in the future force approximately 2,000 military personnel equally divided between operational personnel of the kind currently employed in Cyprus, and support personnel of the kind currently employed in the UNEF/UNDOF.

Under MOBCOM's present troop rotation policy, a soldier is kept on peacekeeping duty for no longer than six months and is not used again for three years. This has worked reasonably well up to now, but a shrinking manpower picture is beginning to shorten the span between rotations. In reality, the three-year rule requires that five times the number of men employed in peacekeeping at any one time be kept available for rotation, or a total of 9,600 ** They, too, need logistic backing and transport and communications organization, which raises the on-hand figure to 11,000 — or 1,000 more than MOBCOM's entire sharp end.

The rotation situation became so critical in 1975 that MOBCOM was finally forced to leave many essential operational billets in Canada unfilled in order to provide a peacekeeper. This "multi-tasking" had a devastating effect on logistics positions, which are the grease that keeps a modern army rolling. "When a telephone lineman is sent from Kingston to the Middle East, or a cook from North Bay," said a concerned defence official, "there is

*UNEF: UN Emergency Force on Israeli-Egyptian border;
UNDOF: UN Disengagement Observer Force on Israeli-Syrian border.
**(based on 1,600 troops: 1600x5 equals 8,000, plus 1,600 on duty equals 9,600)

nobody to plop into his vacant job in Canada. Everybody must simply work longer hours and cover for the guy who is not here. The efficiency of units in Canada becomes degraded and, after a while, overwork starts to affect morale."[59]

General Dextraze explained it this way in November 1975: "The troops we have in Canada are multi-tasked. They are tasked for priority one, two, three and four, and the tour that our people do in Cyprus is a six-month tour . . . (but) the troops we send over there (means) that Canada is deprived of them immediately. Of course, they are always available. We can always bring them back if we have an emergency, in the country or elsewhere, when we need them."[60]

Ironically, Canada's peacekeepers of all people are poorly equipped to handle an explosive situation should it burst around their ears. Aside from a handful of armoured personnel carriers, most of the millions of dollars worth of equipment ordered for the "peacekeepers of the seventies" by Paul Hellyer, never found its way into their hands, or was cancelled by the Trudeau government. They have no air support, field artillery or means of escape from a dangerous situation. *That* will be rushed from Canada in time of need. However, that is not always possible, as Canadian peacekeepers in Cyprus found out in 1974.

In July, Canada's 500-man contingent on the Mediterranean island suddenly found itself in the middle of a savage shooting war between Greek and Turkish forces. When the smoke cleared, two Canadian soldiers were dead and eighteen wounded. Military officials generally concede that casualties probably would have been higher had it not been for the lucky presence of the Canadian Airborne Regiment's 1 Commando, on Cyprus duty at the time. Throughout the weeks of fighting in and around the capital city of Nicosia, Canadian troops manned observation posts, fought several heavy engagements to protect civilians and preserve their own lives, and performed a great many peacekeeping and humanitarian functions.

In late July the hard-pressed 1 Commando was reinforced from Canada by its No. 2 Commando and members of the Lord Strathcona Horse. However, *it took more than a week to airlift the 500 reinforcements and their field equipment.* Nicholas Stethem, a former Captain in the airborne, explains some of the strategic difficulties faced by Canada's brave but ill-equipped peacekeepers:

> The Canadian Airborne Regiment, basically unsuited to the task, cobbled together a force for routine duty on Cyprus, and when war broke out on the island it was reinforced by the remainder of the regiment from Canada. The result was a cohesive, highly trained force that was accustomed to working together. Both before and after the reinforcement they performed well.
>
> I would like to think that it was the presence of soldiers from my old regiment that saved the day when the Turks were about to take over Nicosia airport, for example. Unfortunately, the truth is that without the support of modern British tanks, artillery, anti-tank weapons and modern jet fighters — a Canadian support group could not have provided the same up-to-date equipment. The spirit was definitely there but the big guns had to be borrowed.[61]

The situation is different in the Middle East where most of Canada's 1,200 troops, including fifty servicewomen, are noncombatants. Skilled tradesmen, they provide communications, air transport and logistics support for the UNEF in the Sinai Desert buffer zone and the UNDOF in the battle-scarred Golan Heights between Syria and Israel. The force was airlifted there in late 1973, following resumption of hostilities between Arabs and Israelis. More recently, in April 1978, ninety Army communication specialists from Kingston, Ontario, were sent to Lebanon following Israeli raids into that border country.

They will provide the vital communications links for the newly created UN Interim Force in Lebanon. Regrettably, Canada was forced to turn down a UN request for more men and limit the ninety communicators' stay in Lebanon to six months because, explained External Affairs Minister Don Jamieson, "We're stretched pretty thin as it is."[62]

Should the Canadians become caught in the middle of a war, they could not protect themselves like the combat troops in Cyprus. After 1969, when domestic concerns shaped many training programs, the Army's service corps were no longer taught how to fight; that was reserved for the combat trades. Stethem tells why this could spell disaster for Middle East peacekeepers:

> Troops were scraped together from all over Canada, and thrown into the middle of a war that could turn hot again at any moment . . . Unfortunately, the trades necessary for this type of work have not been considered "combat" trades since the reorganization of the sixties. Thus, in digging for personnel, many men were recruited who had scarcely any experience in the field. Men who had only fired a rifle once a year since their early training were expected to work in an area where bullets were flying . . . in many cases it was a matter of the unqualified leading the untrained. The recent decision (1975) to send women to the Middle East is, I suspect, less motivated by considerations of equal employment than by a critical shortage of qualified manpower.[63]

In addition, the length of time it took to airlift the first wave of troops to Egypt makes it difficult to believe General Dextraze's claim that "we can always bring them back if we have an emergency . . . when we need them." It took two Boeing 707s and fifteen Hercules more than ten days, working round the clock, to airlift 481 troops and 151 vehicles to Egypt. The second wave of 500 troops took two weeks to deliver.[64] The forces have five

Boeings and twenty-eight Hercs. In this light, it would seem that in a real emergency at home or abroad the forces would have a tough time getting their sun-baked peacekeepers to where they were needed most, and on time.

FADING AWAY

The slow disintegration of the Canadian Airborne Regiment offers a microcosm of the problems besetting the over-stretched resources of Mobile Command.

The airborne is still Canada's elite military formation, the roughest, toughest and fastest-moving bunch of men in the country. Based in Edmonton since 1970, the airborne can trace its origins back to the fabled "Devil's Brigade" of the Second World War. The paratroopers, resplendent in their sleek multi-zippered jump suits and gleaming calf-high boots, are proud to wear their distinctive maroon beret. They were the first troops into the streets of Montreal during the bleak days of the October Crisis. They distinguished themselves under fire in Cyprus in 1974 when the Turks invaded. In the summer of 1976 they were called on to guard Israeli athletes at the Olympic Games in Montreal. Whenever there was a tough assignment, the airborne usually got the job.

From its permanent home in Edmonton, just five miles from air transport at Namao, the regiment was ideally located for service in the Far North, one of the principal reasons for being based in Central Alberta. Because of its ability to parachute into inaccessible areas, the regiment was "earmarked to provide rescue support in the event of a major air disaster in the Arctic."[65] In addition, the regiment's constant presence in the North on training schemes underscored Canada's claims of sovereignty to disputed northern regions. In May 1974, for example, airborne personnel jumped into a simulated airliner crash site at the North

Pole (planting a flag as well), an emergency situation in which speed would be a critical factor for the survival of passengers.[66]

Organizationally, the airborne is the forces' most self-contained fighting machine. Configured for rapid deployment to Europe in case of war the regiment is really a small brigade which lacks armour support. It contains its own airportable artillery battery, field engineers and logistic units — and everybody jumps, including the clerks.

The men and their families were just getting settled in Edmonton when they became casualties of the manpower and budget squeeze throughout MOBCOM. In 1975, with manpower critically low and the government dead set against allowing a minimal increase, planners at defence headquarters were forced to scrounge for more combat personnel from within existing units to offset attrition at the "sharp end." After squeezing the last outpost dry, eyes were reluctantly cast toward the airborne. With 1,100 crack troops the regiment became the last pool of highly-trained soldiers readily available to MOBCOM's commander. With peacekeeping commitments on the upswing and recruitment lagging, the internal strain on his understrength units was becoming severe. In the fall of 1976, after months of speculation, the government announced the airborne would move east the following year. General Dextraze described the decision as part of "a military appreciation of a military requirement"[67] because he could get no more men, but there was a widely held conviction that the government planned to break up the regiment and redistribute its men to other units.[68]

"If they move the regiment," agonized the *Edmonton Journal* in 1976, "what will happen to the thousands of people in the North who depend on the airborne's services? The airborne provides emergency service in the North when there are storms, floods or fires . . . it flies in emergency supplies . . . and it does all the search and rescue operations."[69] It was airborne troops who rescued the ill-fated downed Arctic flier, Martin Hartwell, in 1973. When the move was announced the Edmonton Chamber of Commerce cabled the Government: "The presence of French-speaking troops in western Canada enhances the Federal Government program for bilingualism. It would be a retrograde step to relocate the regiment, particularly to a francophone area." But the need for warm bodies in the centre was too great to resist.

The move had a shattering effect on the regiment's morale, particularly when the men thought their unit would be split up. The regiment's French-speaking 1st Commando (250 men) was to be stationed at Uplands air base in Ottawa, with the remainder, its "integral airborne combat and service support units" assigned to augment troops at Petawawa, Ontario, 110 miles northwest of the capital.[70] "The men are unhappy about the whole thing," said one of the airborne's officers who was travelling east aboard a service flight in January, 1977. "We liked it in Edmonton . . . we were just getting settled in." Morale was dropping fast, he said, and men were leaving. "Applications for release are already coming in from men who otherwise would have stayed in . . . you know, we are probably the most successful B&B experiment in the Army, and in Alberta!"

At the last moment only good fortune and a full house saved the regiment from developing a split personality. When the 1st Commando arrived in Ottawa there was no accommodation for them or their families, so they were ordered to join the rest of the regiment at Petawawa. The francophone soldiers received the news with joy but realized that a forced separation was still possible. Ironically, the move put an end to the forces' most successful bilingual experiment in Western Canada. The regiment "is unique", noted defence analyst Duncan Fraser on the eve of the move east, "in that it is a quietly functioning example of bilingualism in action . . . that it functions as a bilingual unit in Edmonton says a great deal about some of the unsung bilingual programs."[71]

Aside from damaging morale, the move to Ontario created serious operational problems for the airborne which hinder its quick-response capability. From a military point of view the choice of Petawawa, across the river from Quebec, is puzzling because the base has no airfield capable of handling Hercules aircraft, the regiment's principal means of transport. Two weeks before the move was announced defence officials in Ottawa sent a memo to Richardson's staff, asking: "What is the logic in locating a quick-reaction unit to a base where all-weather flying facilities do not exist and where the closest IFR (Instrument Flight Rules) airport is two hours away?" The reply is not known but presumably in an emergency the regiment would be bused to Uplands, weather permitting, where the men would jump aboard awaiting Hercules. There are other problems, too, some which belie the government's assertion that the airborne was moved to Petawawa because of its excellent training facilities.

To get in the required two practice jumps each month the men are bused to airfields at Ottawa or Trenton, two and four hours away respectively.[72] When the countryside is blanketed with snow the trip can take much longer, and Petawawa is located in one of the worst snow belts in eastern Canada. In Edmonton the regiment was right next door to air transport. Moreover, the Canadian parachute training school is in Edmonton and so are the facilities for drying and packing the parachutes. After a man jumps in an exercise somewhere around Petawawa his chute is bundled up and sent all the way to Edmonton, repacked, then returned to Petawawa.[73] Time consuming, yes, but at least the men are jumping. For a few months during the budget freeze they could not even do that. When elements of the airborne returned to

Edmonton from Cyprus in December 1974, they were not allowed to practise parachute jumping because fuel shortages had grounded the Hercules.[74]

Today the airborne faces an uncertain future, particularly since its gutsy commander put his career on the line in an effort to save his regiment from destruction. In July, 1978, forty-three-year-old Colonel Jacques Painchaud was the victim of poor journalism and his own keen sense of loyalty to his men. After reading an article in which Danson hinted darkly at the possibility of disbanding the airborne, Painchaud vented his frustration when talking with a former soldier turned journalist. Thinking he had a sympathetic ear, Painchaud explained how the move east and the air of uncertainty had taken its toll on his men's morale. He was surprised a few days later when his remarks appeared in the July 10th edition of the *Ottawa Citizen:* "I am expected to be an example of loyalty to my men," he said, "but what can I say when our big chief (Danson) is making statements like the one last Thursday. It's irresponsible. If he continues like that he should be replaced."[75]

Danson had engaged in some fancy kite-flying when he told defence writer Peter Ward that he was "against elite units" because "there's a danger that you will milk your best people from all other units for such elite formations."[76] Tory defence critic Allan McKinnon and DND insiders knew Danson's comments were designed to draw reaction to a plan to disband the airborne and redistribute its men to under-strength units.[77] Painchaud, sitting on tenterhooks in Petawawa waiting for the axe to fall, reacted emotionally to Danson's remarks and paid a heavy price.

Less than a week after his intemperate comments hit the papers Painchaud was hauled on the carpet by defence chief Admiral Falls, on orders from Danson, and relieved of his command. Painchaud, who always jumped first when his men were parachuting into unknown terrain, appeared before Falls on crutches because he had just broken his ankle in a jump with his regiment.[78] It was to be his last jump. He was assigned a desk job in Ottawa. When the colonel returned to Petawawa to clean out his desk, he said his goodbyes in private to a tearful gathering of Canada's toughest soldiers. They were not pleased with Danson.

"He loved us," said one paratrooper. "He said what everybody felt — and those dictators in Ottawa took him away from us. Now they're going to send some yes-man who will sit with his hands over his eyes while they break up the regiment."[79]

The reaction of one airborne officer was similar: "We have seen the government put the needle in just before shoving in the sword. The rumours last week were the needles and the commander's reaction was that of a fighting man, a goddam good fighting man. We will have to wait and see if the government shoves in the sword next."[80] Danson was quick to assure the regiment that he had no plans to disband it, but the problem still remains: MOBCOM is critically short of men to perform its assigned peacetime tasks properly and the airborne is the only readily available source of trained combat personnel.

Should the airborne be broken up, as it probably will be in the next few years, the remnants of the Canadian Army will have lost their last "elite" combat group, along with their proud tradition and irreplaceable skills. After the premature death of the crack Black Watch and Queen's Own rifles, the passing of the airborne would be a heavy price to pay for denying MOBCOM the few thousand more men it needs to strengthen its fading ranks.

# 4 NATO

Trudeau's NATO policies have blackened Canada's good name in the councils of Europe. As a charter member of the Atlantic Alliance, Canada always met its collective defence commitments on time and with fighting iron. But in only ten years Trudeau has earned Canada the reputation for being a leech on Europe's back; a nation determined to share in the benefits of Alliance membership, but unwilling to pay a fair share of the costs involved. Recent statements by the Prime Minister indicate he is not prepared to correct the situation.

## OUR BOYS OVER THERE

From 1951 to 1969, Canada stationed more than 10,000 crack troops in Europe as part of NATO's first line defences against the threat of a Soviet invasion of Western Europe. Well equipped and rated the best soldiers and fliers in the Alliance, Canadian land and air forces were a symbol of Canada's post-war belief that in matters of national defence, its borders started at the Rhine. Both forces were equipped with tactical nuclear weapons.

During the sixties the 6,000-man 4 Canadian Mechanized Brigade Group (4 CMBG) manned a chain of nine forts strung along the Iron Curtain in northern Germany, just east of the industrial

Ruhr Valley. As part of the British Army of the Rhine, they were poised to absorb the first shock of a Soviet onslaught across the North German Plain and, if possible, to counter-attack. The mechanized brigade was backed up by Canada's six squadrons of supersonic CF-104 "Starfighters," which were designed to deliver nuclear counter-strikes deep within Soviet territory. Together they were not a big force, but the Canadians were highly regarded by friend and potential foe alike as a force to be reckoned with. But the situation today is very different.

SUICIDE BRIGADE

Canada's present NATO force is the smallest, weakest and most insignificant military contribution to the Alliance. In 1970 the Canadian force was slashed to 5,000 men and moved to bases at Lahr and Baden-Soellingen in southern Germany, 400 miles from their front line forts in Westphalia, to assume a morale-sapping reserve reconnaissance role. The air component was cut to three Starfighter squadrons and both land and air elements traded in their nuclear weapons for conventional hardware.

The force is too small and ill-equipped to perform its assigned reconnaissance and counter-attack role, and lacks the capability even to defend its own bases against direct conventional attack. Its only value is political — to give Canada a voice in the councils of Europe (and, hopefully, trade advantages) at the cheapest possible price. The tiny force contributes to the illusion of Alliance solidarity, but strategically it is a suicide brigade.

In light of known Soviet strategic doctrine in Europe, the conversion of the Canadian force from nuclear to conventional weapons made poor military sense. Since the late sixties, when NATO adopted the doctrine of flexible response based on a strong conventional capability, Warsaw Pact forces have steadily massed huge quantities of tanks along the Iron Curtain for what western officials believe would be a lightning armoured assault. Without tactical nuclear weapons, Canada's small mechanized group would be next to useless in their counter-attack role — or in any role — in a theatre dominated with atomic weaponry. But the government repeatedly rejected recommendations from NATO and its own advisers either to re-equip the brigade with tactical nuclear weapons or to increase its conventional capability.

In 1974, Dr. George R. Lindsey, chief of DND's Operational Research and Analysis Establishment in Ottawa, the closest thing defence has to a 'think tank,' wrote: "The forces of the Warsaw Pact . . . are designed for a short . . . blitzkreig offensive. In fact, many calculations show them reaching the Rhine in a matter of a few days, unless NATO escalates to the employment of nuclear weapons, and even if nuclear weapons are employed, it is by no means certain that the balance will be swung in favour of NATO."[1]

The Brookings Institute confirmed Lindsey's analysis, noting that "a fundamental assumption on the part of the Russians is that any major conflict in Europe between the U.S.S.R. and NATO would probably encompass an early use of nuclear weapons, and certainly the ever-present threat of their use."[2] Tactics manuals issued to Warsaw Pact forces also indicate that Soviet strategy in Europe is based on a surprise armoured thrust preceded by selected nuclear strikes.[3]

To some, Trudeau's decision to leave a skeletonized, non-nuclear force in the middle of a potential atomic battlefield was close to treason. "If we believe in supporting NATO," wrote R. S. Malone, "surely our obligation is to do so with the most effective weapons that are available to us. To do otherwise and allow our troops to remain in a position of danger, inviting advances through having inferior weapons is the height of hypocrisy and immorality . . . *In past history, leaders who have negligently left their troops exposed to needless danger have been impeached on the grounds of morality, treason and stupidity."*[4]

The men of 4 CMBG see their situation in a similar light. "We're a token suicide force," said a tank captain at Lahr in 1976. Another said, "we'd be wiped out in two days in the event of hostilities."[5] General E. L. M. Burns, Commander of the 1st Canadian Corps in Italy in 1944 and now a visiting professor at Carleton University, said "they *are* a token force with no military capacity to produce an effective contribution to the Alliance ... or defend themselves. I think it would be better if they were brought back up to the level they were before." In 1977, Canada's total military contribution in Europe accounted for less than one percent of NATO's combined land and air forces, and that small number operates at less than peak efficiency.

When 4 CMBG was restructured and reduced to 2,800 men, the fine tuning of its internal combat and support elements went out of balance, which in turn precipitated a steady decline in its over-all efficiency and combat capability. It is now the only land force among NATO units committed to an active combat role which is manned and equipped for peacetime operations. This is a result of manpower cuts throughout the forces and particularly in Mobile Command, which is too starved of troops to keep its NATO brigade up to strength while having to provide a steady supply of men for peacekeeping rotation.

In 1976 General Dextraze admitted at a closed meeting in Ottawa that 4 CMBG needed at least another 1,500 men immediately to bring its fighting elements up to normal "peacetime operating levels." The manpower shortage in the vital logistic sub-units, such as transport and supply, is so bad that more than 150 positions are now being filled by Militia personnel. In fact, the brigade is so short of support personnel that it can no longer conduct its important full-scale Fall exercises "without the assistance of several hundred members of the Militia," reported one observer in 1976, "who were flown out here to drive vehicles and help man guns. The result is a five-days-a-week affair, instead of a fighting unit capable of responding to calls on a twenty-four-hours-a-day, seven-days-a-week basis that war demands."[6] This trend is now accelerating as the shortage of trained combat troops worsens. In addition, more than two dozen women participated in the Fall '76 exercises, the first time they had been used in a simulated scheme. The trend is continuing.

In the event of hostilities, the brigade group would be hard pressed to carry on even if it managed to survive a brief encounter with a small enemy force, because it lacks its important tactical reserves. They are back in Canada, engaged in unspecified domestic work, but are ready to be airlifted to Europe if needed. The fighting end of the brigade looks like this:

two infantry battalions of three companies each;
one armoured regiment of two tank squadrons;
one artillery regiment with three gun batteries;
one squadron of combat engineers with two field troops.

General Dextraze has fought unsuccessfully to rebuild the currently unbalanced 4CMBG which, he maintains, "must be organized at the fighting echelon as follows:

three infantry battalions of four companies each;
one armoured regiment with three tank squadrons;
one artillery regiment with three batteries of guns;
one squadron of combat engineers with three field troops.[7]

"History and our experiences on past conventional battlefields," he said, "have demonstrated that if one is to fight and expect to survive, one must be organized to fight with a credible war establishment. 4 CMBG in its present configuration will require augmentation if it appears that it is about to be committed to action."[8]

General Bell believes, "the present brigade presents many serious tactical problems . . . The chief (Dextraze) wants the brigades there to be made into regiments, which they're not; and the missing pieces mean that if the brigade is ever pressed into battle it could not function effectively in that battle because it would be deficient in tactical reserves — they are as important as the main strike force. Without them the brigade cannot train or fight properly. They are vital to all strategic movement, forward and backward."

### THE RAMBLING WRECKS

Militarily, 4 CMBG was the worst equipped force in the Alliance until February 1977, when thirty-five rented Leopard tanks replaced its primary piece of heavy fighting equipment, the twenty-five-year-old Centurion tank. (The brigade's new tanks start arriving this fall.) The Centurion, aptly named the "agony wagon" by the men who used the tank, was the joke of the Alliance and a rolling museum piece. A few days after the 1971 White Paper sounded the tank's death knell, an eager officer at NDHQ rushed this memo through channels: "The Canadian War Museum is interested in obtaining a Centurion tank as a permanent exhibit," and suggested one could be found among those "soon to be returned from duty in Europe."

The brigade's armoured regiment, the Royal Canadian Dragoons (RCD), operated two squadrons of sixteen Centurions each but barely twenty were mechanically fit for even limited duty. The rest, along with a few rusting hulks in nearby sheds, were steadily cannibalized for spare parts. Another sixteen tanks were held in "ready reserve" back in Canada for the Dragoon's phantom third squadron, but it would have taken weeks to get them to Europe because they were too heavy and bulky to be airlifted. They would come by sea.

·"We're supposed to be ready to reinforce allied units," said a tank captain in Lahr, "but most of our tanks can't make it out the main gate without breaking down."

For training exercises in northern Germany, 4 CMBG was forced to beg tanks and artillery from American and German forces to conduct a feasible operation. In 1972, a fifteen-year tank veteran complained: "Our Centurions should have been replaced long ago. You go out on manoeuvres and they break down in the first fifteen minutes and you have to wait three days for spare parts."[9] It took three days to change a Centurion's motor compared with less than an hour for modern American and German tanks.

While mechanics strained and invented new ways to keep the Centurions alive, tank drivers practised the infamous "Mexican shift" to keep them under control. This tricky procedure (trying to get back into gear after the tank went into neutral) compensated for worn transmission linkage that could no longer be replaced because of age. During Exercise "Certain Trek", in October 1975, a driver lost control of his tank when he missed the shift — which had to be made before the tank was rolling too fast. The Centurion careened wildly down a steep hill, injuring three crewmen who jumped from the runaway monster. One suffered paralysis from a spinal injury. On the first day of the exercise, another Centurion blew its motor while warming up for an attack. Its driver was badly burned.[10] Tankers told many such stories. Nor did the Centurions stack up very well against the competition on either side of the Iron Curtain.

Aside from mobility problems, the Centurion's firepower was poor compared to the Russian T-62 tank, the principal armour of opposing Warsaw Pact forces which was rapidly being replaced by a bigger model. The Centurion's top speed of twenty miles an hour stacked up badly against the thirty-five miles an hour average of other allied tanks.

The agony wagons were also insatiable gas gobblers (a quarter of a mile per gallon) with a range of 118 miles per tank — not far enough to reach their assigned battle areas in the Central Front region from home base. According to a DND report in 1972, the Centurion's average cruising speed on paved roads was fifteen miles per hour and less than ten cross country. "Leaving the Centurion over there," said a retired colonel, "was a stupid, wasteful political mistake. It was a cheap trick to play on men who are sitting in the hot seat and exposed to a better equipped enemy."

The brigade has fewer than 250 operational M113 A1 armoured personnel carriers.[11] In theory, these tracked troop carriers are "designed to provide ground forces, particularly the infantry, with increased mobility and protection not found when operating on foot."[12] In reality, however, they are death traps. Purchased by Hellyer, they are totally inadequate for use in the potentially "hot" atmosphere of the Central Front.

In the event of nuclear hostilities, the men in them would be cooked in seconds. The Soviets' basic armoured infantry carrier (the BMP) is heavily armed and equipped with positive pressure air-conditioning as a precaution against nuclear, chemical or biological warfare. It is basically a self-contained mini-fort, providing its nine infantrymen with every conceivable protection. American, British and German troops enjoy similar protection. The Canadians? According to Army officers, the following 1976 report accurately tells the story:

> Its (APC's) alloy skin, only one-quarter inches thick, is not even proof against a rifle bullet, let alone heavy machine guns. Most

of them carry a single .50 calibre machine gun in a mounting so inadequate that it is almost a dead loss. It wobbles so much that it is hopelessly inaccurate and in most of them it cannot be used in the horizontal mode without getting out of the vehicle.

The M113 is not equipped for nuclear, chemical or biological warfare and cannot, like its Soviet counterpart, be used as a fighting vehicle in either the mobile or static mode.

Basically, it is a fast, highly-manoueverable soft-skinned box on tracks that offers defence against splinters and against small arms when fired from a distance.[13]

The APCs are so poorly armed that they cannot provide their troops with important covering fire. In 1975, Nicholas Stethem, a career officer serving with the brigade in Europe, explained why. "Before leaving this force I saw a final example of 'modernization.' There had been rumours for some time that our APCs were to be re-equipped with more modern weapons." They "were fitted with an out-of-date .30-calibre Browning machine gun modified to take modern 7.62mm NATO ammunition. Our allies are now equipping their personnel carriers with such weapons as 20mm cannon, or at very least, with modern types of machine guns, and we had hoped that we might get something similar. *What we finally received were old .50 calibre machine guns from storage where they had been placed as obsolete years before.*"[14]

The brigade's fleet of twenty-four Lynx tracked vehicles provide all-important reconnaissance capability. They are advance "observation posts," operating ahead of the main force to watch the enemy and report his movement. What they report, or fail to report, could mean life or death for the entire main brigade, whose commander relies on the information to make tactical decisions. The Lynx, however, suffers from many of the same deficiences as the APC, of which it is a modification, and is totally inadequate for its role.

The Lynx has no protection for its three-man crew against nuclear or biological warfare and, in light of a secret DND report on its faults, it is hard to agree with the government's claim, contained in a public relations handout, that it is "a highly-agile . . . armoured vehicle capable of amphibious and rough cross-country operations . . . (and) easily adaptable to airborne operations."

For more than a year in the early 1970s a team of DND technical specialists examined the Lynx's capabilities and potential as a direct fire-support replacement for the tank, and as a "command and reconnaissance"vehicle to operate with a tank, which is its present assignment. It failed on both counts. On February 12, 1972, the team's report explained reasons:

its .50 calibre machine guns were obsolete and lacked necessary anti-armour . . . capability"

at 23,000 pounds, it was *not airportable* and only one could be airlifted in a Hercules after considerable modification

it was too slow (forty mph) and lacked sufficient cruising range (325 miles) to be effective

its diesel engine was too noisy for reconnaissance work

its reverse speed was too low and it could not turn in its own length

it was already past its "mid-life" and was becoming costly to maintain[15]

As a tracked vehicle, the Lynx handles scouting assignments amid the wooded hills and dales of central Germany. On-road reconnaissance missions are left to the brigade's two dozen Ferret scout cars, which are twenty-four years old and useless. They were declared obsolete in 1972 but reprieved in 1973 when the Centurion was resurrected. Like the other armoured vehicles, the Ferrets are vulnerable to nuclear or biological agents, have a top speed of about fifty miles an hour — not much more than new Russian T-72 tanks — and have only a light machine gun.

The artillery picture for 4 CMBG is getting brighter after several dark years when it was left with a tiny arsenal of obsolete weapons. Artillery, light and heavy, provides critical defensive capability against a variety of land and air threats. Fortunately, the brigade's heavy artillery — eighteen 155 M109 self-propelled howitzers — are relatively new and rated as excellent *conventional* pieces of medium artillery. Purchased by Hellyer in 1968, they are deployed in three six-gun batteries with the 1st Regiment, Royal Canadian Horse Artillery. Unfortunately, they are the only heavy artillery fire-support assigned to the brigade and have already been rendered semi-obsolete by newer weapons.

Allies and Warsaw Pact forces use similar weapons and are presently acquiring scores of multi-missile rocket launchers. These weapons "could effectively multiply our firepower by a factor of six," wrote one Canadian military expert, and "would help close the gap between artillery support afforded Warsaw Pact units and that afforded to our own."[16] Because of the Howitzers' limited firepower, they are grouped and fired together in "six packs" to maximize effectiveness. In a potential nuclear theatre this is considered unwise because "the increased destructive capability available to the enemy will make the diversion of our artillery equipment a necessity," said the expert, "lest a lucky blow immobilize an entire battery."[17]

Air defence artillery is considered a high priority by NATO planners, but the Canadian brigade's arsenal does not reflect this concern. Until 1975, the brigade had no anti-aircraft weapons whatsoever, apart from a few dozen obsolete 106mm recoilless rifles which, noted John Gellner in 1973, were "hardly suitable for defence against modern jets . . . if, heaven forbid, Canadian forces had to go into battle, their only protection against air attack would be to duck."[18]

In 1973, Defence Minister Richardson promised that Canadian troops in Europe would be equipped with British-made Blowpipe surface-to-air missiles by 1974. However, because of budget restraints, the intended order of 150 was cut to 100. The last of seventy Blowpipes arrived in Europe this year, with the others allocated to the Combat Training Centre at Gagetown and CAST combat group.

The brigade plans to use its portable Blowpipes to defend bases against enemy aircraft. In a pinch, they can be used to support troops operating in the field. A few dozen Blowpipes are held at Baden-Soellingen, home of Canada's three squadrons of CF-104 aircraft, to back up what is considered the worst defended air base in Europe. Main anti-aircraft defence of the base consists of several batteries of eye-sighted 40mm "Boffers" (ack ack guns), which were removed from the aircraft carrier HMCS Bonaventure in 1970. They are about twenty-five years old and are rated as highly effective against propellor-driven aircraft flying at less than 250 miles an hour. Normal ground attack speed of supersonic Soviet fighters is about 500 to 600 miles an hour.

An Army major said "the Blowpipe is a good air defence weapon, but our troops there (in Germany) need at least 100 or 125 of them to be really effective . . . sixty-odd is not enough to provide even minimal protection to tankers and foot soldiers against air attack." He also believes the government's reluctance to purchase more Blowpipes is due to the high cost of ammunition. One Blowpipe missile costs $8,500 compared with $15.50 for one round of Boffer ammunition. "You can imagine why the Boffers are still there," he said.

### 1 CANADIAN AIR GROUP — THE "WIDOWMAKER"

Canada's three squadrons of Starfighters at Baden-Soellingen are considered next to useless as fighter bombers, their role since being stripped of nuclear rockets in 1972. Attached to the 4th Allied Tactical Air Force, whose area of responsibility is the sky over southern Germany, the thirty-six operational Starfighters are expected to "provide close air support for armies assigned to the Central Army group, including . . . 4 CMBG during operations."[19] But their conversion to fighter bombers makes poor sense. Aside from being misemployed, their all-important firepower was reduced to dangerously low levels — the lowest of any tactical aircraft in Europe. They too, are a token suicide force with no strategic significance.

"Using a Starfighter to drop iron bombs is like using a Cadillac to pick up garbage," said a former air base commander in Germany. "It's stupid."[20] A Starfighter pilot added: "My father in World War II carried a bigger payload — in a lighter plane."[21] AVM Cameron agreed: "As a low-level fighter the Starfighter is a bust. It takes a terrible punishing at low levels, where air stress is greater and fatigues the metal on the old birds . . . SACEUR* and our own air people told them (government) not to use the 104s in this role, but they got nowhere . . . and their armament is pathetic."

The Starfighter carries one ancient 20mm cannon, a variety of anti-personnel bombs (little ball bearings, etc.) and up to three 500-pound bombs. Incredibly, the Starfighters were not all converted for their new role until 1977; for five years many lacked adequate self-defence capability against other aircraft. "It is inconceivable," wrote John Gellner in 1975, "that it would take four and a half years to install Vulcan 20mm cannon with gun-

*Supreme Allied Commander Europe, NATO's top military chief.

sights, (and) under-the-wing pylons for external stores . . . because money was allocated so slowly."[22]

In its present role, the Starfighter carries too little armament to be of much value as an attack aircraft, nor can it protect ground troops. With only one big machine gun mounted in the nose, it cannot protect itself from aerial attack from rocket-equipped Soviet aircraft. "You might go screaming in for an attack," said Major George Lowes, "but if anything caught you in there, you'd never come out. There isn't another air force using the 104 in a conventional ground attack role because it's too good an aircraft for that."

Another problem, said Major Lowes, is visibility. "For a ground attack the pilot is almost blind. The cockpit's forward visibility is limited because you don't need it, which makes it hard for the pilot to see the ground. It was designed for supersonic attacks, therefore you've got a long-range-ahead visibility but you can't look up and down and see very much. What the hell are you gaining by sending in a 104 with a couple of cannisters of napalm and guns? It will scare the hell out of the enemy, but that's all."

The Starfighter is also dreadfully old, costly to maintain and dangerous to operate at low levels. Purchased by Canada in the early 1960s, the aircraft is the oldest fighter in NATO, requiring an average of forty-five maintenance hours for each hour in the air — twice the recommended level for combat aircraft. And with large air intakes designed for high-level flying, the Starfighter has a deadly tendency to suck birds into its engines during low-level operations. Dubbed the "widowmaker" by its pilots, more than fifty Canadian Starfighters have crashed in Europe in the last dozen years killing more than fifteen Canadians. Close to twenty of the crashes were caused by errant birds.[23]

Richard Rohmer, Chief of Canada's Reserve Forces, said in an interview, "the Starfighter was not designed for its present role.

There are difficulties with it. It's an old airplane and it's being flown by a lot of brave guys. And on top of that it deserves replacement like yesterday." The government has no plans to replace the aircraft until at least the early 1980s, when a new fighter aircraft is scheduled to come into service.

FLIMSY BIRDS
The air group also operates a dozen small Kiowa helicopters to support operations of 4 CMBG. Based at Lahr, the 444 Tactical Helicopter Squadron was created in 1972, after Cabinet rejected DND recommendations to acquire a small fleet of heavy, well-armed helicopters for use in combat zones.[24] The tiny Kiowa is unsuited for its role as bloodhound of the brigade group, sniffing out the enemy ahead of the main force, because it carries no weapons and lacks armour protection. "A pistol shot is enough to get us down," complained a Kiowa pilot in 1976."[25]

The Kiowa was designed and built in the United States as a light observation helicopter for environmental services. It is a favourite of radio journalists for making their morning traffic report. Canada is the only NATO force which commits the Kiowa to scouting missions in a nuclear combat zone, where the enemy carries several excellent anti-aircraft systems. "Using Kiowas is such incredible nonsense," said AVM Cameron. "The men in them haven't got a chance in hell of surviving a twig thrown in anger, let alone a rock." The official government release on the Kiowa says it was acquired for, among other things, "armed reconnaissance," but its only weaponry is provided by the co-pilot, who rides shotgun with an automatic rifle.[26]

The Kiowas bloodhound "tracking" role is to clear the way for infantry and armour on the move, hedge-hopping ahead of the main force to pinpoint the enemy and pass the word back for artillery and air action. However, because they are weaponless and dreadfully slow — 115 miles an hour — they operate in tandem "suicide teams." One advances while the other sits and watches. Then, when all is clear, the latter moves up, scans his area, pronounces it clean, and sits to watch his companion repeat the manoeuver. If one of the choppers encounters the enemy — "one of the best ways to do this is to get shot at," said a pilot — the other runs back to report, if he makes it.

## THE POLITICS OF NATO

The story behind the decline of Canadian Forces in Europe from an elite combat group to a demoralized rear guard is one of political image making, shifting priorities and penny-foolish budgets. When Trudeau came to power in 1968, one of the first major issues facing his new government was the question of what armed forces Canada would continue to base in Europe as part of NATO's defences. The commitment to maintain 10,000 troops abroad expired at the end of the following year and NATO planners were anxious to have a quick answer. To find one, the Special Task Force on Europe was set up, which included senior representatives from several government departments. In February 1969, the group recommended that Canada maintain its present military posture in Europe. But Trudeau was not satisfied. Struggling as he was to control federal spending, he wanted a new policy to reflect his own known lack of interest in NATO, and to save money.

For a fresh view, Trudeau had his personal aide, Ivan Head, assemble a group of known critics within the bureaucracy of existing policies. Called the nongroup by some, it recommended that Canada reduce its NATO forces to 3,500 men but remain "in NATO to make its voice heard in the Western Alliance as it sought a new relationship with the Communist bloc."[27] The group also urged the de-nuclearization of Canadian forces in Europe, particularly the squadrons of CF-104 nuclear attack aircraft, as a goodwill gesture to the East. They pointed out that the aircraft were offensive rather than defensive weapons and thus could be perceived as a threat to Warsaw Pact forces.

The Defence and External Affairs ministers were shocked at the suggestions. Both Leo Cadieux and Mitchell Sharp had recently blessed the Task Force position to maintain the status quo in Europe and they angrily rejected suggestions to debate the unofficial nongroup report in Cabinet. "The attitudes reflected at this time by the people close to Trudeau" said General Bell, "were against the nuclear role and mechanized force, against any real fighting capacity, and the tensions that developed generated a requirement for something different."

That something different led to a compromise: Canada would stay in NATO but its forces in Europe would retire to a reserve role and drop their tanks and nuclear weapons. The government explained that besides saving money, such a force would bring its European brigade into line with NATO's strategy of "flexible response," which sought to maintain enough conventional (non-nuclear) military strength to contain a Soviet armoured attack and thus prevent escalation to nuclear war. De-nuclearizing the Starfighters, Ottawa rationalized, meant "they will be more readily available to some of Canada's hypothetical defence needs."[28] But tanks were another matter. They were the heart of conventional land defence in Europe, and the primary conventional weapon of the Warsaw Pact nations.

Ironically, the decision to drop tanks was endorsed at this time by General Jean Allard, then CDS, who sat in on latter nongroup discussions. "People blame him," said General Bell, "and in a way I think he's blameable. But he was bringing these ideas in at a time when he knew his political masters were saying 'no tanks.' So he said let's develop something on the basis of no tanks. He then developed the concept of a lightly equipped, air-transportable force, which had been part of some of our field force proposals before . . . but not at the expense of losing the main battle tank."

The government's aversion to buying tanks was based on a belief that they were strictly offensive weapons, thus needlessly provocative, like the nuclear-equipped Starfighters. It was also known that the crop of "bright boys" around Trudeau were aghast at the prospect of ever seeing tanks used in Canadian streets to maintain order, so tanks were out. AVM Cameron claims "no tank" memos bearing the PM's signature flowed from the East Block as early as 1968. Generals hotly disputed the reasons given for dropping the tank, pointing out its offensive and defensive merits were necessary for survival on a battlefield, but they were overruled by Cabinet.

"Canadians are asked to believe," wrote Cameron, "that since there is no military need for tanks in Canada, their purchase for use with the Army in Europe is not justified."[29] Others pointed out that the tank was the heart of the combat arms team, and without its support, infantry soldiers faced certain destruction from enemy armour.

"To say that the soldier's survival on a battlefield is no longer relevant, because Canadian foreign policy will never again ask him to tread there," wrote General E. A. C. Amy, one of Canada's most brilliant tank commanders and now Colonel Commandant of the Royal Canadian Armoured Corps, "has to be a political gamble at best . . . in all conscience they cannot make the decision to scrap the tank."[30]

Trudeau disclosed the nub of his new NATO policy on April 3, 1969. Due to the "magnificent recovery of the economic strength of Western Europe," he said, the government intended to "bring about a planned and phased reduction of the size of the Canadian forces in Europe." The news surprised NATO allies who had not been consulted, and reaction was swift. Britain, Germany and others complained that Canada was letting the Alliance down at a time when Soviet forces in Europe were growing rapidly. In May, NATO's top brass were not amused with the Canadian proposal when it was discussed by the Alliance's defence planning committee, as General Dextraze explained in a secret memo written in 1973:

> When the structure of 3,500 was presented subsequently to NATO, SHAPE* and AFCENT**, it was received with considerable dismay and numerous aspects were criticized, particularly the unusual assumption that other Allies would provide the airlift and that the flank role for the battle group (in Canada) was therefore not feasible. Moreover, they stated that such a force, on the basis of size, composition and particularly lack of armour, was unsuitable for a role on the Central Front.[31]

U.S. General A. J. Goodpaster, SACEUR, flatly objected to Canada's force reduction proposal as "incredible." During the summer of 1969 Ottawa and NATO officials huddled on both sides of the Atlantic to find a mutually acceptable force structure. Cabinet approved a revised structure on August 13, after less than twenty-four hours of consideration.

Leo Cadieux announced the details on September 19. Canada would cut its force to 5,000 men, and ship both land and air components to bases in southern Germany, where they would assume a reserve reconnaissance role. The army contingent was slashed to 2,800 men, gave up its Honest John nuclear missiles but kept its Centurion tanks. The six squadrons of CF-104s were cut to three and stripped of their nuclear rockets. Two were converted to a conventional strike role, the other for photo reconnaissance.

*Supreme Headquarters Allied Powers Europe
**Allied Forces Central Europe

But Cadieux's announcement made it clear that "these are interim force. For the post-1972 period we plan to equip a land element in Europe . . . as a light airmobile force and convert the air element to a conventional armed ground support reconnaissance role."[32]

The 5,000-man force "was a compromise proposed in August by General Dare,"* said General Bell, "and it's still there. It was approved very quickly in Cabinet without much argument and was presented to SHAPE and his representative. It retained the battle tank and enough men to satisfy SHAPE's demands. But it was still couched in the terms that it would only be there — and in that configuration — until the air-transportable future equipment came in. Of course, it never did."

In the Fall of 1970, with protests over the force reduction still ringing on Parliament Hill, flat cars of Canadian armour rolled southward from Westphalia leading the 5,000 Canadian troops and 10,000 dependents to their new homes in the picturesque Black Forest region of southern Germany. After a year of settling in, both air and army components were partly de-nuclearized and ready to perform their new reserve roles, the details of which were spelled out in the 1971 White Paper.

*Defence in the 70s* contained few surprises, but it did appear to seal the fate of armoured regiments on both sides of the Atlantic. It explained that in order to promote internal compatibility of weapons and to make most of Canada's military effort relevant to domestic missions, the mechanized brigade group would shed its tanks and assume a new "airportable" tactical reconnaissance role in the Central Region. The Centurion tank was to be replaced by a "light, tracked, direct-fire support vehicle (DFSV)." Donald Macdonald believed that "the result will be an enhanced

*Lieutenant-General Michael Dare, then VCDS

compatibility of Canadian and European based forces, and lighter, more mobile land force capable of a wide range of missions."[33]

### POST-72 FORCES

The rather cavalier manner with which Canada appeared to treat its NATO commitment was interpreted by many as the first step toward eventual withdrawal from Europe. Militarily, its interim force was so small that many doubted it should be left there at all.

The land force boasted only 2,800 men of a grand total of 580,000 in the alliance in Europe. It was equipped with thirty-two operational Centurion tanks, 375 M-113 armoured personnel carriers, eighteen M-109 155mm howitzers and a few hundred twenty-year-old trucks. At Baden-Soellingen, sixty kilometers north of Lahr, the three Starfighter Squadrons flew thirty-six aircraft and kept eighteen in reserve. "Canada's current NATO contribution is hardly impressive in a military sense," wrote author Colin Gray, and "common sense suggests that the post-1972 ground force contribution will be of even less value to SACEUR than is the current one."[34]

In a sense, Canada's military posture in Europe was being shaped as much by a desire to look less warlike to home opinion than from sound strategic reasoning. Aside from a wish to keep tanks out of Canada, the government viewed them as an unwarranted expense at a time of military cutbacks and frozen defence budget. Despite protests from allies and its own generals, Cabinet was determined to replace the Army's last Centurions with light armour by 1974. Only one hurdle remained: obtaining SACEUR's blessing to do it.

In September 1971, less than a month after publication of the White Paper, defence planners had already decided to replace the tank with the British-made Scorpion tracked armoured reconnaissance vehicle. The Scorpion was a pale shadow of a tank, weighing nine tons compared with the Centurion's fifty-six, and carried two small calibre guns as main armament. Tankmen paled at the thought of trading down to Scorpion, but the government seemed firm.

In March 1972, a team of officers from NDHQ went to Europe, presented SHAPE with a plan of the post-1974 light armour reserve force and requested endorsement. A month later, while the plan was being studied, DND's information department quietly prepared a press release for the minister's signature announcing the "purchase of 131 Scorpions ... for $42 million."[35] It was never released. General Dextraze, then CDS-designate, argued strongly against buying the Scorpion or any similar vehicle for use in Europe, where "it could not function effectively in the heavily armoured environment of the Central Front." In a memo to Defence Minister Edgar Benson, he expressed "dismay" that his "views did not halt the procurement action process . . . while SACEUR's proposals were still being examined."

But Benson was not dismayed. In late July he visited London to sew up the Scorpion deal, holding press conferences as he toured the country. "As far as the military is concerned," he said, "we'd like to have the Scorpion and we have been negotiating a contract and talking about numbers." He hinted that a contract would be signed within a month.[36]

The government moved quickly on the Scorpion deal because its armoured regiments on both sides of the Atlantic were driving decrepit twenty-year-old armoured cars and scout vehicles. The Scorpion would replace most of them. Under the never-released plan, Canada would buy 131 Scorpions — sixty-one for the NATO brigade and seventy for use at home. In Canada, sixteen Scorpions would replace tanks at the Combat Training Centre to train crews bound for Europe. The rest would be scattered from Valcartier to Calgary "for reconnaissance and operational support of the Canadian Forces in preserving control over the security within the national territory of Canada and areas of Canadian jurisdiction"[37] — the very reasons why Cabinet had rejected buying more tanks.

Benson's apparent anxiety to clinch the Scorpion deal quickly can perhaps be explained by a memo sent to him in February by the VCDS, Lt.-General A. C. Hull. The memo said the need for Scorpions in Europe was particularly urgent because "the tracked squadrons of the reconnaissance regiments will be unable to fulfil the assigned mission without a DFSV. The present armament of scout vehicles and the support weapons in the regiment are not adequate to deal with many of the targets which may be encountered during operations . . . and with the planned phase-out of the Centurion tank in 1974, the requirement for a DFSV becomes almost vital."

While Benson was parlaying in London, SACEUR let Canada know what his experts thought of Canada's post-1974 force structure. General Dextraze explained in a 1973 memo:

> On July 21, '72, SACEUR, based on studies by commanders and his staff, forwarded detailed comments regarding the deficiency in armour and engineers and requested further consideration of Canada's decision on the tank question. He also stated that neither the U.S. nor F.R.G. (Federal Republic of Germany) forces with whom 4 CMBG was associated on the Central Front could provide tank support to augment the light Canadian force because there were insufficient tanks available to perform the covering force and forward defence tasks.
>
> These findings have also been confirmed by AFCENT who has stated that at the stages of battle when reserve formations are committed it could not be counted upon that tanks would be available to

support the Canadian light force since all other armour would have been committed earlier in the battle.

AFCENT . . . further states that the proposed light post-74 force based on SCORPION without light support:

a) would be unable to perform the primary role of the reserve which is counter attack;

b) could not perform a covering force; and

c) could hardly be considered able to perform in its secondary anti-airborne/heliborne role.[38]

It is apropos to point out here, the general concluded, "that Canada in requesting to be relieved of its forward defence role, *volunteered* for the reserve role, on the Central Front."

SACEUR's unflattering response to the Canadian proposal left Ottawa with two basic choices: keep their tanks in Europe or withdraw altogether. Reluctantly, in the Fall of 1972, Cabinet initiated secret negotiations with Germany for possible purchase of the Leopard Mark I battle tank, a highly-rated descendant of the mighty Panzers. At the same time, General Dextraze slipped unannounced to Germany to examine first-hand the potential battle area of the Canadian land brigade. "This I did in secrecy," he wrote, "with the commander of CFE and SACEUR and confirmed amongst other things that . . . the Canadian proposal based on Scorpion without tanks was not militarily viable on the Central Front."[39]

On his return to Canada, General Dextraze recommended that Canada not buy the Scorpion and extend the life of the Centurion tank until at least 1976. A ground force equipped with Scorpions would have little chance to "survival," he said, adding that if the decision to keep the Centurions appeared as a reversal of government policy, "it can logically be explained" because of strategic changes in Europe since the 1971 White Paper. The main change was the alarming buildup of Warsaw Pact armoured forces, which by the beginning of 1973 enjoyed a tank superiority of more than three to one over NATO units — 7,750 vs 25,000 — and the gap was growing in the Soviet Union's favour.

General Dextraze pointed out that a decision to kill Scorpion would save more than $40 million for a weapon of limited utility, as well as increase Canada's stock in NATO. It would also "have important effects on morale within the Forces because it would reflect professional recognition of the continued and increasing Warsaw Pact armoured threat on the Central Front where our forces are committed." Failing this, he added, "I therefore ask myself what political benefits could Canada gain by remaining in the NATO Alliance as a contributor to the requirements of the Central Front?" In July 1973, James Richardson announced the Scorpion was dead and extended the Centurions operational life to 1976.

Following the Centurion's resurrection, Canada's NATO policy drifted aimlessly for more than two years. The contingent in Germany waited in vain for news of new equipment, which was held up by budget restraints and ministerial uncertainty. From top to bottom, the force's equipment was decaying from "fair wear and tear." The air group needed new fighters to replace the aging CF-104s. The infantry waited for their new TOW and Blowpipe portable field artillery designed to counter tanks and aircraft. They were still using obsolete recoilless rifles that had been phased out of every other allied command years earlier. But most of all, they awaited word on a tank.

Ottawa's interest in re-equipping its NATO warriors was rekindled in mid-1975, following Trudeau's tour of European capitals in search of a "contractual link" with the common market countries. In May, he attended NATO summit talks at Brussels, where he agreed that "as long as the Warsaw Pact continues to increase the size and preparedness of its forces, we cannot afford to leave them unopposed." When his words were not followed by promises of more military support, European allies made one thing perfectly clear. "Increased economic ties with Europe," said NATO commander General Alexander Haig, "would be tied with a NATO knot."[40]

Europe expected Canada to beef up its meagre forces as a tangible expression of Alliance solidarity, and as a down payment for any special trade links with Europe. At the Brussels talks, according to Canadian officials, German Chancellor Helmut Schmidt bluntly told Trudeau: "No tanks, no trade." Tory MP Allan McKinnon said, "Trudeau was told in no uncertain terms that if he wasn't ready to keep up Canada's NATO forces and re-equip with modern weapons, he couldn't hope to play in their economic game."[41]

Throughout the summer of 1975, NATO officials prodded Canada to start replacing its obsolete Centurion tanks and Starfighters in Europe. In the Fall, U.S. Secretary of Defence, James Schlesinger, made a whirlwind visit to Ottawa, where he told the government the time had come to start paying its way and beef up its NATO forces. In September, after much pleading, Canadian officials attending NATO talks in Copenhagen managed to quash the following damning paragraphs from appearing in an official report:

> The situation regarding the Canadian military forces is far from satisfactory; the strength of their active forces has been reduced and no decisions have been made to replace major items of equipment for the land and air forces which have become obsolete.
>
> A review of the Canadian Forces this year is likely to substantiate even more strongly the picture of Canada as a country determined to participate actively in and influence the political councils of NATO, anxious to maintain her economic links with Europe, *but unwilling* (their italics) to make a contribution to alliance defence which is

commensurate either with these aspirations or her economic strength.[42]

On November 27, 1975, Canada suddenly rediscovered Europe. With the light switched on by common market allies, Richardson announced that Canada would provide either new or overhauled main battle tanks "to ensure that our army contingent in Europe possesses the necessary up-to-date equipment fo fulfil its assigned tasks beside our NATO partners." Starfighters would remain in service, pending future review of the entire air picture. However, only the NATO brigade would get tanks.

"Richardson originally wanted to re-equip all the armoured corps with new tanks," said AVM Cameron, "but the boys in Cabinet said 'nyet'; they didn't want any tanks in Canada."

Ottawa's sudden recommitment to Europe, albeit small, appeared to some critics as a repudiation of its 1969 declaration that defence began — and ended — at home. Richardson heralded this new direction in defence thinking on November 15, 1975, when he told a group of officers: "Where is the threat? The threat is largely in Europe, on the Central Front. The threat is not as we see it, in North America."[43]

At the same time, Richardson revealed the gist of new thinking that would shape Canada's NATO defence policy in the near future. Having dropped a nuclear role, and in the face of growing Warsaw Pact forces, Canada would remain in NATO and strengthen its conventional forces "to prevent the western democracies from getting into a position where we have to choose between unacceptable alternatives: nuclear war or capitulation. We don't want to be in that position, therefore we must have a strong conventional capability. We must have what is described as flexible response."

To provide that flexibility in Europe, Richardson, in October 1976, finally persuaded Cabinet to buy 128 Leopard C-1 tanks, instead of rejuvenating the Centurions. Portable field artillery was ordered for the infantry, and new trucks slowly began replacing the ancient fleet which had become almost useless.

### THE TANK FACTOR

From a military perspective, the original decision to drop the tank had created serious training and operational problems for Canada's small NATO brigade. But more than that, the delay in buying a replacement has cost at least an extra $100 million for what military experts believe will soon be an obsolete tank.

In the Fall of 1972, when it appeared the Scorpion deal was dying, Canada secretly reopened negotiations with the German producer of the Leopards, Krauss-Maffei of Munich, and a bargain was struck. "We could have bought at a guaranteed delivery price," said General Bell, "160 Mark 1s with first year spares for about $320,000 a copy . . . and had them delivered within two years. By the Fall of 1974 we would have been converted."

The $55 million deal included a minimum 40 percent "buyback" clause. But Canada balked because "we were just coming out of the freeze," said General Bell, "and Cabinet didn't think we could afford tanks at this time. We tried very hard but they wouldn't budge."

Four years later Canada ordered 128 Leopard C-1 tanks at a cost of $187 million, which included the rental cost of thirty-five training tanks until their own arrived between late 1978 and 1979. Fifty-seven tanks will go to the Dragoons in Germany; a few dozen will be used as trainers at Gagetown and CFB Borden, Ontario. The remainder will go into reserve.

Ironically, after so long a delay, the government's eleventh hour rush to buy tanks was ill-considered and may prove costly.

In a desire to pacify European leaders on the tank question, James Richardson tipped Canada's bargaining hand while negotiations were still going on. He held a press conference in Europe and "announced to the world that Canada was accepting a 30 percent buy-back," said R. J. Hauser, a senior Canadian official involved in the bargaining. "This single act succeeded in cutting the legs right out from under the negotiators," he said, "all at a time when other options were still open." The result: "About $120 million worth of orders for Canadian industry went right down the drain."[44] Canada finally managed to wangle a provisional 40 percent, with less attractive terms.

Despite appearances, tank problems for the NATO brigade are not over — they are just beginning. In its zeal to put shiny new hardware on display in Europe, the government bought a tank that will be the oldest and most outgunned machine in Europe in a couple of years. The Leopard 1 series has been in production since 1965, and is now being phased out. The Germans will soon introduce the much superior Leopard II. Many DND advisers urged the government to lease C-1s until the Leopard IIs appeared at which time Canada could have purchased a tank that was sure to remain up-to-date for at least a decade. "After seven years of waiting," said MP Allan McKinnon, "we could have waited another year or so to get the best available."

In a few years the Leopard C-1 will be the most under-gunned tank on either side of the Iron Curtain. With a 105mm main gun, the Leopard will have a tough time coping with the 122mm weapon of its main opponent, the Russian T-72 tank, and a bigger one is on the way. In 1976, Canada rejected purchasing the British Chieftain tank for $1 million a copy because it was too expensive. Iran has since bought 1,200 of them for $900 million, including spares and logistic support.

The government also refused to wait for the appearance of the

Leopard II or American XM-1 tank because neither would be available until the middle 1980s, and Canada's requirement for a new tank was more immediate. Both tanks are equipped with 120mm main guns and will be available before 1980. In addition, the Chieftain, XM-1 and Leopard II will come equipped with the greatest advance in tank design in 50 years, Cobham armour.

Defence officials claim the Cobham armour, named after the south England town where it was developed, will offset the numerical superiority of Soviet tanks in any potential land battle. Unlike conventional tanks, those built with Cobham armour can withstand direct hits from all known anti-tank weapons and other tanks. After extensive field testing in England, British Defence Minister Roy Mason announced: "By the time this armour is in general service it should have quite an effect on the military balance of land forces in Central Europe . . . for there is no firm evidence that the Russians have developed anything like it."[45] By the mid-1980s it is expected that most tanks operating with NATO armies will enjoy the protection of Cobham armour, except Canada's.

Seven years after their strategic withdrawal from northern Germany, Canadian troops appeared ready to resume a more active role at the nation's first frontier of defence — the Rhine. The 5,000-man "interim" force waited for word of more men and for the tools to do the job. Only two questions remained unanswered: would they arrive in time, and would they be enough?

## THE FUTURE
Present defence policy does not plan to increase the number of men in Europe, despite recommendations by top military officials in Canada and NATO to at least restore the brigade's missing

tactical reserves. Richardson, in his secret memo to Cabinet, urged the government to maintain the air component at its present level but to revitalize "the land component by raising armoured and artillery equipment inventory to full regimental levels (fifty-seven gun tanks, eight non-gun tanks and twenty-four self-propelled guns) and a consequential increase in the present manning level and, if necessary, *an adjustment in the level of planned augmentation required to bring the brigade to combat strength.*"* As this could only be achieved by raising the total force manpower ceiling by a few thousand, it was rejected. However, the government replied later with a sleight-of-hand compromise called the Canadian Forces Europe Augmentation Plan, which Defence officials admit is unworkable.

The plan calls for Canada to leave sufficient tanks, guns, vehicles and other weapons in storage at Lahr and Baden-Soellingen, so they can be used by reinforcements flown from Canada. In 1977, General Dextraze outlined how this would affect 4 CMBG:

"Its tasks and peacetime organizations will remain unchanged except that a third squadron of tanks and a fourth battery of M109s will be located in Europe. Personnel to man these will come from Canada annually, as part of the CFE Augmentation Plan."[46] The plan also calls for an additional company for each of the two infantry battalions and an additional field troop for the field engineer squadron. But there are serious flaws in this plan.

First, the plan presumes that in the event of war Canadian troops could miraculously remain in possession of their bases until reinforcements arrived to use the stored equipment. This is a

*This recommendation was endorsed by the entire Steering Group of the Defence Structure Review Board. It was the number one recommendation in final submission to Cabinet.

naive assumption in light of known Soviet strategic doctrine, which would see the bases pasted with nuclear or chemical weapons prior to rolling over them with columns of armour.

Second, even if nuclear weapons were not used, Canadian troops are too poorly armed to prevent capture of their bases by conventional enemy forces. Dr. Lindsey points out that "the present NATO forces . . . cannot hope to contain a full-scale Warsaw Pact armoured offensive without deep withdrawal."[47] Which means Canada would be forced either to destroy its stored weapons — including eighteen Starfighters and nineteen tanks held in reserve — or lose them to an advancing enemy, before reinforcements could arrive. Considering the limited airlift capability of the forces Air Transport Group, it appears almost certain that reinforcements for the NATO brigade would never leave Canada in time to be of any strategic value.

The augmentation plan can only be viewed as a cosmetic concoction designed to convince Europe that Canada is ready and willing to play an active role in collective defence — but at the cheapest possible price.

Finally, the arrival of the new tanks will make no significant difference to the brigade's firepower, although they will reduce the horrendous number of maintenance hours lavished on the Centurions. The Leopard's British-made 105mm main gun is identical to the Centurion's, although the Leopard has a modern laser range finder linked to a ballistic computer that should ensure quick first-round hits. And without the companionship of a new tracked reconnaissance vehicle, the Leopards will be forced to double in both scouting and attack roles, which increases considerably their chances of being destroyed before being used in the vital counter-attack role. Unless 4 CMBG receives more men and equipment to become a properly balanced unit, it will remain Canada's suicide brigade in Europe.

The Trudeau government's lack of a realistic NATO defence policy has left Canada's 5,000 soldiers and airmen in Germany —and their families — needlessly vulnerable to growing dangers. In their present form, Canada's European forces are of minute military value to the Alliance. The decision to denuclearize the force and ship them south to a reserve role could be defended had they been armed to perform that role. But they were not, and that is a problem.

Regardless of political desires, it is only logical that Canada's NATO forces should be armed with weapons similar to those possessed in vast quantities by the potential enemy. Morally, there is no justification to commit troops to fight a better armed opponent simply because our primary arms — tanks and nuclear weapons — have been ruled "incompatible" with Canada's domestic defence needs, and are, therefore, denied to front-line troops abroad.

For years Trudeau's puzzling NATO policies have angered allies and embarrassed Canadian diplomats and soldiers in Europe. He would say one thing and do another; re-affirm his commitment, then cut his forces in half. When he finally decided to buy new tanks, many allies took it as a sign that Canada was again ready to play a greater military role in Europe, or at least bring its small brigade up to full strength. That now appears to be a false hope.

On May 30, 1978, Trudeau spoke to the NATO summit in Washington and committed Canada to increase defence spending to help offset Russia's mushrooming military might. "In seeking to improve the reality of our security," he told delegates, "we must maintain the balance of deterrent strength."[48] To achieve this, Trudeau gave Canadian endorsement to the Alliance's plan to pour some $80 billion (the U.S. picking up half the tab) into armaments over the next decade to meet the spiralling arms buildup of the Warsaw Pact. "I support the concept and the objectives of the program," he said.[49] Under the spending plan, Canada would be required to increase its defence spending by an additional 3 percent a year over the next fifteen years. This works out to about an extra $100 million annually. Trudeau was praised for his commitment, which appeared to seal Canada's return to the NATO fold. But when he returned to Ottawa, Trudeau explained somewhat triumphantly that he had not really committed Canada to anything, and certainly not to spending more money on defence.

Opposition Leader Joe Clark and some of Trudeau's own back-benchers were confused. When Clark pressed the Prime Minister to clarify Canada's position on the matter, Trudeau gave the Commons a demonstration of fancy semantic footwork similar to that which had apparently fooled NATO delegates days earlier. Clark wanted to know if supplementary estimates would be introduced to provide for the increased defence spending as a result of the well-publicized pledge made at the summit talks. He pointed out that the proposed $100 million (or 2.8 percent) of the defence budget already approved for the current fiscal year, was earmarked to replace old equipment in the forces. It had nothing to do with the NATO pledge. Would there be any more money?

No, there would not be another $100 million, or anything. Trudeau explained that because any money spent by Canada on defence could be considered to be for NATO, there was no necessity to increase the defence budget above the ceiling decided in the new spending formula.[50] But that 12 percent ceiling had already been lowered by a handshake agreement between Danson and Treasury Board, which means the forces will be making unexpected budget cuts next year to compensate. When Clark said the prime minister was telling the country that "Canada entered into no new agreements to NATO at the meeting just concluded," Trudeau did not reply. Meanwhile, in the pretty Black Forest country, their families sleeping in rows of brightly-painted PMQs, the men of Canada's tiny and ill-equipped NATO brigade keep close watch on the Iron Curtain, praying it never parts.

# 5 AIR COMMAND AND NORAD

The Trudeau government first presided over the slow disintegration of Canada's military air elements, then changed its mind and laid plans to renew and expand the role of Canadian air power into the next decade and beyond.

### GUARDING THE SKIES
When Trudeau came to power in 1968, the Royal Canadian Air Force had passed into memory two years before. It had been dismantled by Hellyer, who had tied some of its parts to other service elements which required air support and left the two principal components to continue their missions as two separate functional commands. Air Transport Command (ATC) carried on as the forces' airborne freight and passenger service, and the Air Defence Command (ADC) remained Canada's contribution to the North American Air Defence Command (NORAD), the continent's shield against surprise attack from the sky.

NORAD was born in 1958, when Canada and the United States joined forces to provide a joint air defence system. It was an age when many people imagined fleets of Soviet nuclear bombers streaming down over the North Pole to attack the military bases and cities of North America. NORAD's mission was to detect enemy bombers and destroy them. Failsafe and Strangelove had become household words.

By 1962 the basic surveillance system was in operation. It consisted of strings of radar stations which stretched across northern Canada and Alaska, linking up with the Greenland-Iceland-U.K. Line. These silent sentinels were backed up by more than a hundred squadrons of fighter/interceptor aircraft whose mission was to seek and destroy enemy bombers before they could deliver their deadly payloads. For those that got through, nuclear-tipped rockets waited in underground silos to be activated at the push of a button. North America was guarded from bomber attack. Then missiles appeared.

By 1968 the bomber threat was being eclipsed by the appearance of ICBMs (inter-continental ballistic missiles) and SLMBs (submarine-launched ballistic missiles). NORAD countered with more sophisticated radars, satellite-based sensors, outer space detection systems and a host of other innovations. More than ever was NORAD an important part of North America's shield against all forms of attack from the skies, and ADC was an integral part of it.

This chapter focuses on ADC because it represents the "sharp end" of Canada's airborne defences, which are assigned to defend the nation's sovereign airspace. The Maritime Air Group and "10 TAG", assigned to other commands, have been discussed earlier. The air transport wing and tiny Air Reserve do not figure significantly in the future scheme of things.

ROLES AND RESOURCES
The chief of ADC is also the commander of the 22nd NORAD Region, the only one of the eight regions with headquarters in Canada. From a massive computer complex sunk deep in granite-like rock at North Bay, Ontario, the commander directs air de-

fence of close to 2.5 million square miles of Canadian and U.S. territory. The region embraces eastern Canada from the Ontario-Quebec border, the top of the New England states and the entire Canadian North. Western Canada and a small corner of the Maritimes are protected by American interceptors under control of command centres south of the border.

In 1968, the commander's manpower resources consisted of about 11,000 regular airmen, a small but adequate number to handle ADC's inter-locking mission: detection and tracking of objects in Canadian airspace, and their interception/identification *and* destruction if required.

The first assignment was handled by technicians who manned twenty-two DEW (Distant Early Warning) Line search radar stations in the Arctic, and twenty-seven long-range radar sites of the Pinetree Line, which stretched across Canada at roughly the 50th parallel from Gander, Nfld. to Holberg, on the northern tip of Vancouver Island. At Cold Lake, a newly opened satellite tracking station provided warning against surprise missile attack from space.

The interception and destruction capability was provided by three all-weather fighter squadrons equipped with fifty-six supersonic CF-101 "Voodoo" aircraft: one at CFB Comox, B.C.; another at CFB Bagotville and a third at CFB Chatham, N.B. A training squadron of Voodoos at Bagotville could provide backup support, if required. The Voodoos were equipped with nuclear-tipped air-to-air missiles capable of destroying bombers.

ADC also maintained fifty-six BOMARC-B nuclear surface-to-air interceptor missiles of dubious value split equally between two squadrons — one at North Bay, a second at La Macaza, P.Q. There was an electronic warfare squadron based at CFB Ottawa, equipped with old CF-100 and T-33 jet aircraft, which provided realistic training for the Voodoo squadrons and radar systems against electronic and other types of jamming. Both fighter models were scheduled for retirement in 1975. In addition, ADC was responsible for providing training pilots and ground crew for Canada's Starfighter pilots serving with 1 Canadian Air Group in Germany.

Trudeau's major policy statement on defence in April 1969 did not change ADC's primary mission, although NORAD was promoted in the list of defence priorities to a share of first place. Sovereignty was a popular phrase of this period as Canada moved confidently ahead into its second century and nationalists began calling for increased Canadian control of NORAD facilities located in Canada. Only the 22nd Region was under direct Canadian control and no Canadian general had ever been commander of the joint defence system. What would happen if Canadian officers were on duty during a "delicate" situation between the U.S. and Soviet Union in which the Canadian government did not want to get entangled? The nationalists wanted some changes.

POLITICS OF NORAD

The 1971 White Paper responded to rising nationalist concerns by promising more Canadian control of its own airspace. "Although from a strictly air defence point of view," it said, "it may make little difference whether the aircraft is Canadian or U.S., from a national point of view the government believes that normal peacetime identification should be performed by Canadian aircraft."[1]

For a start, 417 Training Squadron at Cold Lake, which flew Starfighters, was quickly assigned the interception/identification role on the prairies, and Voodoo squadrons at Bagotville and Chatham were assigned to handle the Atlantic "corner" and parts of Labrador.

The White Paper recognized that while Soviet missiles had all but replaced bombers as the single greatest strategic threat to North America, bombers could still be used in a follow-on attack role behind them. In future, Canada would maintain enough interceptors to ensure peacetime control of its own airspace and to prevent bombers from destroying the U.S. second-strike capability, and hence preserve deterrence. The Paper also announced that the two BOMARC-B squadrons would be retired and the missiles returned to the United States.

While the NORAD radar system was important militarily, it was also valuable to Canada as a means of maintaining normal peacetime surveillance of its vast northern regions. With an ever-increasing volume of transpolar air traffic to watch, the government wisely believed that a greater degree of civil-military cooperation in air traffic control was the most logical and cost-effective approach to the problem.

In addition, the NORAD radar system was getting uncomfortably old and left large areas of Canadian airspace uncovered. DEW Line coverage, for example, was limited to about 200 miles north of the line itself and was blind to low flying aircraft in many areas. To correct the fault, Canada was looking at two systems being developed in the U.S. — AWACS (Airborne Warning and Control System), a Boeing 707 converted into a flying radar station with immense range; and OTH-B (Over the Horizon-Backscatter) radar, which had a range of 2,000 miles. These were still in the prototype stage. In the meantime, the NORAD debate in Canada was far from over.

Many nationalists felt the existence of the joint command eroded Canadian sovereignty because it was primarily controlled by Americans and on Canadian soil. "NORAD is the historical symbol of bigger issues," said Professor Stephen Clarkson of the

University of Toronto, "the integration of Canada economically, culturally, physically and politically in an American-controlled North America."[2] He wanted Canada to pull out.

Others, such as Air Vice-Marshal Cameron, disagreed, arguing that some sort of cooperative defence system like NORAD was inevitable and to Canada's benefit: "By denying the U.S. room to manoeuver in protecting herself (and indirectly Canada) we could help provoke a catastrophe. . . . To reject this modest effort would allow the enemy a free ride with everything in his inventory. We would also lose an investment which has other uses for Canada.

"With NORAD we have representation on defence councils where we can use our wisdom with considerable effect in protecting North America and our national interests. Without it we'd certainly be vulnerable to some very rude shocks in an emergency."[3]

Some of NORAD's benefits to Canada are worth noting. Its elaborate radar and satellite tracking systems enable Canada to perform its unilateral airspace sovereignty duties more effectively than it could manage on its own, and at one-tenth the cost. Under the original pact, Canada gave American aircraft overflight and landing privileges, and the U.S. picked up 90 percent of the cost of maintaining the DEW and Pinetree Lines. That came to well over $1 billion a year, with Canada's share about $150 million.

In addition, Canadian military and political leaders participate in the decisions which may have to be made by the United States in the event of an attack on North America. Without NORAD, there is little doubt that in an emergency the U.S. would overfly Canada and use its bases with or without permission. NORAD allowed Canada a significant degree of say for a fraction of the cost of maintaining the system. The loss of sovereignty associated with participation in NORAD appeared to be more ideological than real. While the agreement did appear like a lord and vassal relationship to some, many viewed it as a gift of geographic necessity, with Canada paying its fair share — 10 percent — in relationship to the ten-times-larger United States.

When the old NORAD agreement came up for routine five-year renewal in May 1973, the government balked. After lengthy debate, it was decided to extend the agreement for two years while Canada reviewed the options: "Running the show ourselves," noted John Gellner, "which would cost plenty, or letting the Americans do most of it, which would infringe on Canadian sovereignty — quite a consideration in this time of rising nationalism."⁴ While options were being considered and a parade of expert witnesses passed through Ottawa to discuss their views on NORAD with the Commons defence committee, Air Defence Command was experiencing its own problems.

## WEARY WINGS

Budget restraints and manpower cuts during the freeze period took a heavy toll of ADC's resources. By 1973, regular force strength had dropped to 8,500 from 11,000 and plans to equip the dozen old Starfighters at Cold Lake with nuclear-tipped rockets had been scrapped, pending review of the NORAD agreement. "From North Bay to the Rockies," said Major Lowes, "our air defences were a joke. The Starfighters at Cold Lake weren't equipped for the interception role the government handed them. It was a flag waving move, nothing more."

The re-equipping of ADC's interceptor squadrons with improved Voodoos had been completed by March 1972. Under a "preferential agreement" between Canada and the U.S. signed in July 1970, fifty-eight old Canadian Voodoos were exchanged for the same number of modernized USAF F-101s. The U.S. also threw in eight extra planes to bring the command's strength up to required levels. The U.S. footed the bill of $28.7 million for the exchange.[5]

Between 1973 and early 1975, the Command's modestly increased budget was flattened by double-digit inflation and the government's $100 million across-the-board cut in defence spending. By 1975, ADC's regular force strength slipped below 8,000 and many of its newly-acquired Voodoos were grounded because of lack of fuel. Major-General William Garton, Commander of ADC at the time, warned: "If the current slowdown in military expenditure continues, we couldn't maintain control of our commitment (22nd Region)." The cutbacks had cut flying time and exercises by half, and if it continued his "personnel will lose their ability in air defence," including pilots and radar operators. "You can't keep doing this month after month after month," he said, without damaging the Command's "ability to fulfil its mission."[6]

AVM Cameron agreed: "The Voodoos spent most of their time on the ground. There was a shortage of pilots and fuel became scarce for training . . . some Voodoo pilots said they were flying less and less each year. That's no way to keep your interceptor pilots sharp."

In 1974, ADC's fleet of sixty-six Voodoos was reduced to forty-four as a cost-saving measure, and because many were virtually falling apart. In June 1975, *only four of the entire Voodoo fleet were operational.* The others were grounded for more than a month while mechanics worked day and night to repair a deadly defect in the planes' after-burners which caused the aircraft to stall at low altitudes. Following temporary repairs, the fleet was further reduced to thirty-six operational planes while pilots murmured about flying "death crates."[7] Plans to replace the

Voodoos were scrapped in the 1974-75 period because of lack of funds.

Saddled with a stable of crippled aircraft and a frozen fuel account, General Garton appealed for more funds and was turned down. To compensate, Canada persuaded the U.S. to reduce NORAD's fourteen annual exercises to four quarterly exercises, then announced: "These exercises (Vigilant Overview) are designed to achieve significant operational economies, including a 75 percent cut in exercise flying requirements."[8]

### THE NEW NORAD

On May 12, 1975, Canada renewed its membership in NORAD for another five years, but with a difference. There was a new emphasis on safeguarding the sovereignty of Canadian airspace by Canadians. In the early eighties, NORAD boundaries will be re-drawn along the 49th parallel. Canada will control two NORAD regions: an eastern one from North Bay and a western region from a new control centre to be built near Edmonton. NORAD will continue to be a semi-integrated command, but based on a more nationalistic footing.

The new pact endorsed NORAD's modified objectives, which replaced bomber defence with protection against any kind of "surprise attack" from the skies. However, a minimum anti-bomber defence will be maintained, because recent developments behind the Iron Curtain indicated that while the threat had receded, it had not yet disappeared, and the presence of interceptors prevented giving the enemy "a free ride."

The agreement recognized that NORAD's advantages outweighed the disadvantages and it called for the development of joint civil-military control systems for national airspace, which meant an end to the duplication of effort involved in building separate military and civilian air control facilities. Canada promoted this aspect of the new pact because it would reduce considerably the cost of building additional air control facilities in western and northern areas.

In September 1975, ADC ceased to be a separate command of the forces and became the Air Defence Group, a part of the newly created Air Command (AIRCOM), which is headquartered at Winnipeg. The creation of AIRCOM was mostly cosmetic, but airmen generally agree it gave them back a sense of identity which was lost when Hellyer broke up the RCAF. In essence, the "Air Force" was reborn. The role of ADG remained the same, including the commitment to provide trained pilots and crew for the air group in Germany.

In 1977, Lieutenant-General William Carr, AIRCOM's first commander, outlined plans to modernize and "Canadianize" NORAD systems which have become ineffective against the latest Soviet bomber — the supersonic Backfire. "Our radar and electronic defence system is getting uncomfortably old," he said, and hinted that the Soviet's new fleet of 100 Backfires could get through NORAD's northern shield by jamming the old radar systems, or by slipping around the uncovered corners.[9] (Since President Carter killed the B-1 bomber program, the Soviets have stepped up production of the Backfire. Defence experts believe they will put at least 400-500 more into service in the next two or three years, effectively reviving the mid-fifties bomber threat.)

Canada plans three distinct changes, starting in the early 1980s. "The first will consist of modernizing the present Pinetree system," said Carr, which means new "equipment that can handle modern enemy aircraft, but also . . . provide the strong sort of radar coverage that will allow civilian air traffic control to come under the system."[10]

Phase Two would extend the improved Pinetree system "along both our East and West coasts," Carr said, which "would have the double effect of blocking off undisclosed entry and giving much better air traffic control for airliners." The vaguely defined third stage "consists of closing down those really old DEW sets and replacing them with much more modern, efficient systems . . . that would give us civil control over the Arctic as well as military. It doesn't exist now."[11] In 1976, the U.S. started Canada on its way with the gift of a multi-million-dollar Baker-Nunn satellite tracking camera, now in operation at St. Margarets, N.B. It complements the one at Cold Lake, also a gift from the U.S.

The new-look NORAD will obviously contain some of the Canadian content that nationalists are looking for, but the cost of acquiring that elusive sovereignty is bound to be much more than the present $150 million paid annually by Canada. The cost-sharing formula has yet to be worked out, and defence planners say it is safe to assume the U.S. will not be as generous as it was during those prosperous days twenty years ago when it agreed to pay 90 percent of the NORAD bill.

The cost of the new western command centre and improvements to North Bay will be close to "$270 million in the next few years," said one defence official working on the projects. After that, annual operating costs would be approximately $100 million if Canada were to assume responsibility for all the other air defence activities in the country now paid for by the United States. In a memo to the Commons Defence Committee in 1975, the Secretary of State for External Affairs, Allen MacEachen, said the $100 million operating figure was based "on the assumption that we would not be required to reimburse the U.S.A. for the value of various air defence facilities which they paid for in Canada (e.g. the DEW Line), and that we would continue to receive without reimbursement various services and information which they now provide as part of the integrated arrangements."[12]

When Canada becomes master of its own NORAD regions, it will also need a fleet of new fighter interceptors to maintain control of its sovereign territory. This was pointed out by the Commons Defence Committee in 1975: Canada "would no longer be able to rely on the United States for the performance in peacetime of certain vital functions, and unless improved or additional interceptors were acquired, Canada would not have the capability to control its entire airspace."[13] In the meantime, the Air Defence Group finds covering the "prairie gap" and the rest of Canada tough going.

GROWING THIN ON TOP

Today the resources of Air Defence Group are inadequate to perform its primary mission of controlling and defending Canadian airspace and it faces the certain prospect of greater responsibilities in the near future. The Command's manpower has plunged to 7,500 regulars and its aircraft are dangerously old and expensive to maintain. "With the increasing age of the Voodoos and Starfighters," General Dextraze said in 1977, "more and more man hours are required to keep these aircraft flying." He pleaded for at least another 1,000 trained men "to see us over this hump until the new fighter aircraft and an improved radar system are introduced," but privately he admitted they are not likely to appear.[14] Officials say ADG requires another 2,000 men immediately to meet operational needs and another 1,000 to 2,000 when the new systems are switched on in the early 1980s. But lack of fighter aircraft is already a serious problem.

Since the Command took over air defence duties on the prairies and in the Atlantic "corner" in 1971, its inventory of operational interceptors has dropped to about thirty-five from seventy-eight.

The three Voodoo squadrons can muster no more than about twenty-five flyable aircraft at any one time, and Cold Lake can field a maximum of ten operational but poorly armed Starfighters. Both planes are close to twenty years old, well past the prime for a fighter and there is still a handful of thirty-year-old CF-100s limping about as "electronic warfare" targets. They were to be retired in 1975, but were reprieved until 1977 to plug the training gap that was to have been filled by then by new planes.

"In order to fill the gap from North Bay to the Rockies," said Richard Rohmer in 1976, "we need fighter squadrons. We haven't got them . . . so the Americans are looking after the territory for us even though we are responsible for it. In any event, we will need more airplanes to do the job. We're taking on command centre functions in Canada and that's fine as far as control centres go, but hardware in the air is another matter."

AVM Cameron is appalled at the present state of ADG. "The idea of not having an integrated air control in North America is beyond belief . . . sovereignty is one thing but, hell, we're down to three squadrons . . . *we can't ever* have less than three squadrons, and the shape they're in is a national disgrace. Whether the government likes menacing fighters is one thing, but we need them just to be able to go up and challenge unidentified blips in our airspace. *We can't give an intruder a free ride,* that's unthinkable."

In 1974, General Carr assessed the Voodoos' capabilities: "The CF-101 provides a limited defence against a modern supersonic bomber; its fire control system is out -of-date, its radius of action severely limited, and with the numbers we own, the CF-101 can provide surveillance and protection over only a small portion of Canada's sovereign airspace."[15]

Two years later, he added: "From an engineering and maintenance viewpoint, retention of the aging Voodoos beyond

1980 would be almost prohibitively expensive because of the growing scarcity of spare parts . . . and high maintenance man hours." The Starfighters were falling apart at such speed through "normal peacetime operations" that it would be impossible to maintain "our commitment to NATO (and NORAD) beyond 1982."[16]

A Voodoo pilot from Comox told me in 1977: "The Voodoos are dangerous to fly. We always have more being serviced than are ready to fly. The guys really don't like to take them up in rough or foggy conditions because they're tough to set down in the soup . . . I wouldn't call them death crates, but maybe flying coffins. They should have been junked years ago."

### PILOT ERROR

Aside from an urgent need for new aircraft, the Air Force is short of jet pilots. This situation is a result of reducing the over-all size of the air element during the initial budget freeze period, which saw pilot training cut in half. By 1974, however, when it appeared Canada planned to take over air defence of its entire airspace for sovereignty reasons, Ottawa hastily ordered the training system to increase its "output from seventy-six to 166 pilots per year."[17] The job of turning out the finished product fell to Colonel Ralph Annis, commander of CFB Moose Jaw, Saskatchewan, site of the force's aircrew selection unit.

The Canadian Forces' fighter pilot is rated the best trained in the world. (Until their planes became too old Canadian pilots usually won NATO fighter competitions.) He belongs to an elite corps within the forces and competition to join the glamorous ranks is keen.

When Colonel Annis was told to crank up pilot production after three lean years, he faced a problem of considerable size — lack of trained instructors. Between 1970 and 1973 the forces lost many Class "A" flying instructors when pilot training was slashed back. They left for better paying jobs in civil aviation. In 1973, the flying school of Moose Jaw had been running at less than 70 percent capacity for three years and most instructors were "C" category, the lowest level.[18]

While the school was trying to lure back top-notch instructors, it hit a snag that diluted the calibre of students and threatens to create a shortfall of jet pilots — the forces' bilingualism program. It is a policy that 50 percent of pilot trainees *and* graduates will be francophones.[19]

In 1976, Colonel Annis explained his dilemma: "Anglophones are standing a block long at the recruiting units and we can still get the high Stanine rating from them that we desire. But the francophones are not waiting at the recruiting unit door and we are taking a lot of them right at the bottom... so naturally there's going to be a little higher attrition rate among the francophones."[20] The Stanine rating is the aptitude test that indicates an individual's suitability (and chances) to become a pilot. A rating between six and nine is acceptable and the anglophone trainees' average in Canada is 7.5; the francophone average is a borderline six.[21]

The force-feeding of francophones through the training system at a time when pilot training is hard-pressed to meet future demands has led to the highest drop-out rate in the school's history — and it is costing a fortune. It costs roughly $400,000 to train a pilot and the cost of the failures is running into millions each year. Undoubtedly, some of this is a result of the B&B caveat. Air Force officials feel this situation could be corrected and a better product produced if admission to flying school was based on merit (as it has been in the past) instead of language, but they have been overruled by political forces at NDHQ.

With pilot training running high gear, only time will tell if there are enough pilots to meet the forces' needs when the long-promised new fighters start rolling in.

**FUTURE FIGHTER**

After years of delay the search for a new fighter aircraft is underway. On March 18, 1977, Cabinet authorized DND to go shopping for 130 to 150 supersonic, multi-purpose fighters to replace its entire fleet of obsolete Voodoos and Starfighters. The price tag: $2.34 billion, and maybe more. The decision guarantees the continuation of ADG as a viable part of NORAD and should help stifle growing American and European criticism that Canada has not been pulling its weight in collective defence, both at home and abroad.

The type of new fighter selected is vital because it will become the Air Force's principal offensive weapon, defending Canada's sovereignty and defence needs through the turn of the century, including its contribution to the NATO alliance.[22] But military planners are worried. Many believe that no more than 130 aircraft will be purchased, a number high-ranking Air Force personnel say is insufficient to handle future roles in NATO and the all-Canadian NORAD. They also fear the badly needed planes will not appear in time.

The first of the new fighters are scheduled to enter service in "mid-1981," but they are desperately needed before 1980, when the present fading fleet will no longer be airworthy. A source close to the defence minister confirmed that new planes likely will not appear before the mid-1980s because of huge budget commitments to other capital items, such as the Aurora, tank and armoured car. He also confirmed the 130 "buy" figure for new fighters. "We had planned for more ... well over 150," he said, but pointed out that the average price of a fighter aircraft has jumped from $7 million to about $20 million in the last four years.

General Carr and his planners favoured different aircraft for use in Canada and Europe, where role requirements are opposite, but they were overruled by Cabinet which wanted to keep costs to a minimum. So the hunt for a single, "multi-purpose" aircraft was on.

There is little doubt that Canada requires a twin-engine fighter for North American air defence. Should an engine fail on northern patrol, the pilot could limp home on the other, saving both himself and the plane. But in Europe, where fighters most likely would be engaged in close combat with enemy aircraft and working in a confined area, a single-engine plane makes better cost-effective and tactical sense.

Cabinet appears committed to the single "all-purpose" fighter because it waited so long to replace Canada's planes. It is the cheapest route to go, although the military roles and requirements in Europe and Canada are different. Some defence thinkers believe the single-plane approach will produce a compromise fighter that will require extensive — and expensive — modifications before tackling its diverse roles; in short, the creation of two fighters from one.

Defence planners are also worried about ADG's future capability to patrol and defend the all-Canadian NORAD regions, an area of close to six million square miles. Government papers indicate that the thirty-six Voodoos will be replaced with a total of thirty new fighters, which would spread Canada's air defenses ridiculously thin.

In 1975, General Garton told the defence committee that ADG required a minimum of "sixty new aircraft . . . to provide adequate surveillance and control coverage in Canadian airspace."[23]

General Carr has mentioned the same number, and defence writer John Gellner claims at least seventy are needed.[24]

Under the new scheme ADG would spread its meagre fighter resources around the country to get more bang for its buck. Cold Lake and Bagotville would become ADG's main operating bases with six fighters each. They would act as maintenance "mothers" for three dispersed operating bases — Comox, Winnipeg or North Bay, and Goose Bay in eastern Labrador — each equipped with six fighters. In emergency, ADG's fighter strength could be augmented by two dozen other aircraft from re-equipped CF-5 squadrons at Cold Lake and Bagotville, which are earmarked to reinforce NATO's northern flank. This plan leaves a total of fifty-four operational fighters in Canada, with an unspecified number in reserve. However, the arrival of the new planes will complete Trudeau's long-sought denuclearization of the Canadian Forces. The Voodoos can still be equipped with U.S.-owned nuclear rockets for air defence of North America. The rockets, stored at various Canadian bases, are the last nuclear weapons in the forces' arsenal. Replacement aircraft for the Starfighters in Germany will likewise be armed with conventional rockets, which defence officials lamely explain can do the job pretty well but without the fallout. General Dextraze was keen on locating a flight of new fighters to a northern base, on Devon or Cornwallis Island, but it appears the small number of aircraft to be purchased will not permit its development.

Fighter deployment in Europe is an unknown factor in defence plans. Only thirty-six Starfighters assigned to 1 Canadian Air Group in Germany are operational. The other eighteen are in reserve, ready for reactivation in times of tension. It is not known if the eighteen reserve planes in Germany will be replaced, or if that role will fall to aircraft held in reserve in Canada. An examination of possible fighter deployment combinations illustrates why a buy of about 200 new fighters is required.

If all fifty-four aircraft in Germany were replaced along with the fifty-four in Canada, the country's total operational fighter strength would be 108 planes. Looking ahead, if there are 108 operational aircraft in service by the mid-1980s, there would be a requirement for more than seventy planes in tactical reserve. Defence Minister Barney Danson has stated that the "new aircraft will serve Canada's sovereignty and defence needs through the turn of the century," but at the present rate of normal attrition, a reserve of even fifty aircraft would be wiped out by then.

For a decade the average rate of attrition for Canadian fighter aircraft due to pilot error and normal accidents has been more than two per 10,000 flying hours a year.[25] Over a period of twenty years, these figures suggest that eighty fighters could be lost in Germany alone. This does not include the potential attrition figures for Voodoos or CF-5s operating in Canada, which would raise the loss figure to well over a hundred. Seen in this light, it is clear why some planners feel that anything less than a fleet of 200 new planes is unrealistic.

"Of course we need more aircraft than the 150 or so they've been tossing around for the past year," said Major Lowes in 1976. "What you hold in reserve is as vital as what you've got in the air . . . 150, you've got nothing left after you've fired the first shot." AVM Cameron agreed: "The present thinking is that we expect the Yanks to cover our backs, which they will. So we'll throw up the minimum number of planes just to show we've paid the price of our sovereignty. It's defence on the cheap."

**THE PLANE**
For more than a year international aviation companies have flooded Ottawa with teams of salesmen trying to land the new

fighter contract. Ottawa hopes to sign a contract in February 1979, and spread payments over ten years to cushion the financial shock on the defence budget. What kind of aircraft will Canada finally choose? The answer is one whose company can provide the sweetest production-sharing deal to help revitalize Canada's ailing aircraft industry. A *quid pro quo* arrangement is central to the final choice and Air Force planners are concerned that economic factors may outweigh military requirements in the final analysis.

Six aircraft are in the running for the milti-billion dollar contract. They are the Grumman F-14 (Tomcat), McDonnell Douglas F-15 (Eagle), General Dynamics F-16, McDonnell Douglas/Northrop F-18 (Hornet), the Northrop F-18L, and the Panavia Tornado from Europe.[26] France's highly-rated Mirage 2000, built by Dassault-Breguet, was among the original six entries but dropped out at the last second.

It is reliably known that the serious contenders in the running are the U.S.-built F-14 and F-15, and the Tornado, a product of British, Italian and German joint engineering. All three are high-performance, twin-engine models with long-range ferry capability, essential in Canadian operations, and all three offer Canada significant economic fringe benefits, particularly the American entries. Ironically, Cabinet had already rejected earlier opportunities to acquire these aircraft at bargain prices, with considerably better economic trade-offs than now appear possible.

In 1976, Canada could have purchased 125 used Tomcats from the U.S. Navy for $7 million apiece. Total cost of the five-year-old planes would have been about $875 million. A year earlier, Richardson informed Cabinet in his secret memo that 100 new F14s could be purchased for $2.4 billion, including spares and trainers. Industry department sources confirmed that Grumman made the offer of 125 used aircraft "as a possible way around the Canadian Forces' tight budget," but it was rejected.[27]

Tory MP Allan McKinnon pushed for the deal because he believed it would have provided the Air Force with an opportunity to "mix" new and used aircraft into a more flexible air defence force for less money.

Until quite recently the Tomcat was considered to be a leading contender. Even its competitors praise the plane's performance and Air Force officers look with envy at the F-14's remarkable radar. For example, other fighters can keep close watch on only one enemy plane or target at a time, but the Tomcat can cover no less than six different targets on its radar, and hold a further eighteen under general coverage. Its air-to-air weapons also shoot farther than those of any other fighter, a distinct tactical advantage when facing a superior number of planes. But now there's a snag. Although Grumman has promised to spend at least eighty percent of the value of the deal in Canada on sub-contracts, the Tomcat's sophistication has pushed its price up to about $26 million apiece, the most expensive fighter in the race. That means a buy of only 130 planes would cost $3.8 billion, clearly too rich for Cabinet.

The offer of 125 used Tomcats for a quarter of today's price may look like a good deal, but it is not as good as the one made by Grumman in 1975. The company wanted Canada to buy 120 fighters (for about $2 billion) and enter into a joint partnership to develop a new version of the aircraft that met Canada's particular needs and which did not land on carriers. "If Canada and Grumman could sell them," noted the *Financial Post* at that time, "we would get a substantial share of all future production. In other words, as the ministers will learn, it is a bit of a gamble but with interesting prospects."[28] Later, there was speculation that

Ottawa wanted Grumman to invest in the new Canadair-de Havilland state-owned aerospace venture as a minority shareholder, but Grumman apparently declined.

The F-15 has been the Air Force's first choice for more than three years. General Carr was pushing for the Eagle when he assumed command of AIRCOM in 1975, and has praised its merits on two occasions in the *Canadian Defence Quarterly*.[29] The plane appears to have the inside track with defence planners, and is a superb performer. Canada could have had it earlier, but Cabinet rejected a deal with McDonnell Douglas in 1975.

The firm offered to sell Canada 120 Eagles for about $1.5 billion and merge its Canadian subsidiary, Douglas Canada, at Malton, Ontario, with the ailing de Havilland and Canadair. Douglas would pick up 40 percent of the stock in the tri-unit enterprise and guarantee to place substantial subcontracts in Canada for the Eagle and its popular airliners, the DC-9 and DC-10, as well as design and build other aircraft.

Industry Minister Alastair Gillespie pushed for the deal: "I think we should order it (Eagle) now," he said in 1975. "If we wait a couple of years we may lose many of the negotiating advantages. So I think we should move now, if we are going to move at all."[30] Cabinet rejected the offer as too expensive. Richardson's memo confirmed that Canada could then have bought enough Eagles to re-equip the Air Force for $1.9 billion.

Today, at $21 million a copy, it would cost $2.5 billion to purchase 120 Eagles, and the company has withdrawn its offer to become the creative junior partner in a new Canadian aerospace triumvirate. "If the Cabinet buys the F-15, McDonnell Douglas will do almost anything to keep Ottawa happy," noted the *Financial Post* in 1975, "but if Ottawa doesn't buy, the company makes it clear that it can see no real future for its Canadian operation."[31] The company now employs about 2,500 people in Canada. A few years ago it employed 7,000.

Finally, the European Tornado is emerging rapidly as the dark horse in an otherwise all-American show. The plane entered competition in late 1976 and recent trial results have delighted Canadian airmen and shocked the big American firms, who thought they had the Canadian deal sewn up. The Tornado is a joint project of the British Aircraft Corporation, the German Messerschmitt-Bolkow-Blohm and Italy's Aeritalia. It would be ironic should Canada choose the Tornado because its conception was mainly a Canadian idea.

In the late sixties, Canada was instrumental in setting up a consortium of six European NATO nations to build a Multi-Role Combat Aircraft (MRCA). Canada wanted Alliance members to develop a new generation of fighter aircraft so they did not always have to buy U.S. planes and mutually to strengthen their domestic aviation industries. The idea caught on and Canada chaired the first meeting of the group, which included Belgium, Britain, the Netherlands, Germany and Italy. But in late 1968, just as a prototype of the new MRCA was getting off the drawing board, Trudeau yanked Canada out of the deal "arguing that spending money on fancy new fighters was just a waste."[32]

That decision, according to Frederick Page, chairman of British Aircraft and of the Panavia consortium, "was a serious blow. We had wanted to work together very much. But Canada had decided to cut its budgets and stay out of it."[33] It was a very costly decision.

The Tornado is just what Canada requires. It is the only one of the six competitors that comes in two versions: a long-range fighter and a ground attack machine, an original Canadian stipulation, which makes it perfect for Canada's NATO and NORAD roles. About 80 percent of all components of both models are the same, which makes it relatively simple to convert to either role. The plane is lighter and cheaper to service than its American rivals and it features modular engine and electrical components, which permit faster replacement in times of emergency. Canadian defence officials have been impressed with the plane's performance, and American firms are clearly concerned.

A big plus factor for the Tornado is that government officials see it as a potential door-opener for closer economic and political links with the European Economic Community, something which Trudeau's forays overseas have failed to produce. Talks between Ottawa and Brussels have been going on for two years, but so far neither side has been able to produce any real results. A buy of 120 Tornados would cost about $2.5 billion, the same as the Eagle. However, Canada's falling dollar in relation to rising German and British currencies, may soon push the Tornado out of reach.

Geography, too, could spell trouble for the Europeans, because the existence of American branch plants in Canada make it easier for U.S. firms to subcontract work back to a subsidiary and the amount of industrial spinoffs offered will be a major factor in deciding who wins the contract. "If we had stayed in with the Europeans," pointed out AVM Cameron, "we would have been building planes for the rest of Europe . . . now we might be buying them and the Europeans won't give us the kind of domestic production deals the Americans would."

DND insiders speculate the Eagle will win out over its main rivals because the Air Force is dazzled by the plane, and because McDonnell Douglas enjoys an enviable old-boy connection with key defence officials in Ottawa, particularly since former Defence Minister Donald Macdonald has now been appointed to its Board of Directors. However, they add quickly that the Tornado is a dark horse that could come from behind if the Europeans are willing to play American-style economic poker with Canadian officials.

**FLAPS DOWN**

After several years of financial throttling, the Air Defence Group is physically too weak to perform its primary mission as guardian of Canada's sovereign airspace. With its manpower and fighter aircraft resources at their lowest point in decades, the group cannot realistically keep under surveillance or defend the top half of North America.

The all-Canadian NORAD is perhaps overdue for a nation more than a century old, but it could be argued that it is also needlessly expensive flag-waving. American domination of NORAD has never impinged directly on Canada's sovereignty and has brought with it many tangible benefits at bargain prices. The present NORAD system is more a gift of geographic necessity than deliberate invasion of sovereignty and Canada still benefits disproportionately. The main concern about the future all-Canadian show is that Ottawa appears reluctant to match its nationalist rhetoric with sufficient hardware to allow ADG to make it work.

Financial restraints and years of ministerial procrastination have left ADG's fighter pilots flying the oldest operational interceptors in the western world, most of which are in an advanced stage of obsolescence. The Voodoos are too old and too few to perform their present tasks properly, yet it appears they will soldier on into the mid-1980s. Delays also mean that Canada will pay at least $1 billion more to acquire fewer fighters than it could have purchased a few years ago, when better deals were available. And if only 130 new planes are bought, then it is probable that Canada will be jet shopping again within twenty years as normal attrition will have wiped out tactical reserves.

In addition, the government's slavish pursuit of bilingualism has watered the ranks of ADG's fighter pilots as well as thinned them. At a time when new fighter pilots are desperately needed, qualified English-speaking applicants for flying school are being turned away in droves while at the other end reluctant francophones are being coaxed into the cockpits. The policy has generated unhealthy tensions between the two language groups, and has contributed to a shortage of pilots. Ironically, a francophone flier works exclusively in English after he graduates, unless posted to a French Language Unit in Quebec.

Today, the sharp end of Canada's Air Force has gone soft. Tomorrow, it appears that unless ADG's strength is increased to at least 1969 levels, Canada's sovereignty of the air will be more a myth than a reality.

## POST-MORTEM

Today, after a decade of Trudeau's mismanagement of the armed forces, Canada stands on the brink of the 1980s as a defenceless nation increasingly dependent on the goodwill and protection of better-equipped allies. As a peace loving country Canada does not desire to have a large and powerful military machine, but it does require a realistic one. It needs armed forces strong enough to defend the nation and to contribute a fair share to collective defence, particularly in these perilous times. Unfortunately, it no longer has them. The Canadian Forces, beaten back by successive volleys of crippling defence policies, are clearly in retreat.

Only Canadians can decide whether their armed forces will be strong enough to meet the challenges of the future, or if they will continue to decline in military capability. That decision must be made soon because time is running out.

## ABBREVIATIONS

| | |
|---|---|
| ADC | Air Defence Command |
| ADG | Air Defence Group |
| AIRCOM | Air Command (the Air Force) |
| APC | Armoured Personnel Carrier |
| ASW | Anti-Submarine Warfare |
| AVM | Air-Vice Marshal |
| CAST | Canadian Air/Sea Transportable combat group |
| CDA | Conference of Defence Associations |
| CDS | Chief of the Defence Staff |
| CFB | Canadian Forces Base |
| CFE | Canadian Forces Europe |
| DDE | Destroyer Escort |
| DDH | Helicopter-Carrying Destroyer |
| DEW | Distant Early Warning |
| DND | Department of National Defence |
| FLU | French Language Unit |
| HMCS | Her Majesty's Canadian Ship |
| LRPA | Long-Range Patrol Aircraft |
| MAG | Maritime Air Group |
| MARCOM | Maritime Command (the Navy) |

MOBCOM          Mobile Command (the Army)
MARPAC          Maritime Forces Pacific
NATO            North Atlantic Treaty Organization
NCO             Non-Commissioned Officer
NDHQ            National Defence Headquarters
NORAD           North American Air Defence Command
SACEUR          Supreme Allied Commander Europe
SACLANT         Supreme Allied Commander Atlantic
STANFORLANT     Standing Naval Force Atlantic

# PEOPLE INTERVIEWED FOR THIS BOOK

Brigadier-General George Bell (ret'd), former Director-General of Plans at NDHQ, now a vice-president at York University, Toronto.

General E. L. M. Burns (ret'd), author, former leader of the Canadian delegation to the Geneva disarmament talks, now a visiting professor at Carleton University.

Commodore Frank Caldwell (ret'd), former commander of the Fifth Canadian Escort Squadron, now Director of Programs for the Navy League of Canada.

Air Vice-Marshal Robert Cameron (ret'd), former air attache to Washington, D.C., now free-lance defence writer.

Michael Forrestall, former Progressive Conservative Member of Parliament for Dartmouth-Halifax East and Opposition defence critic.

Colonel Strome Galloway (ret'd), former Colonel of the now defunct Regiment of Canadian Guards and Canadian military attache to the Federal Republic of Germany, now free-lance defence writer.

Paul Hellyer, former RCAF corporal and later, as Minister of National Defence, the architect of Unification, now columnist for *Toronto Sun.*

Major-General Bruce Legge (ret'd), former Senior Reserve Officer in the Canadian Forces, adviser to CDS on Reserve Force matters.

Major George Lowes (ret'd), aviation writer and former Print News Editor of the Directorate of Information Services at NDHQ.

R. S. Malone, former brigadier-general and war correspondent, now publisher of the *Globe & Mail,* Toronto.

Allan McKinnon, Progressive Conservative Member of Parliament for Victoria and Opposition defence critic.

Richard Rohmer, author, Royal Commissioner and Major-General Reserves.

Rear-Admiral Robert Timbrell (ret'd), former Commander of Maritime Command, now a spokesman for the Maritime Defence Association.

Many still-serving officers and men of the Canadian Forces, who shall remain nameless.

# NOTES TO CHAPTERS

## NOTES TO CHAPTER 1

1. *The Best of Trudeau* (Toronto: Modern Canadian Library, 1972) p. 51.

2. *Foreign Policy For Canadians* (Ottawa: Department of External Affairs, 1970), p. 39.

3. Trudeau, quoted in " 'Suffocate Arms,' Trudeau Urges UN, *Vancouver Sun* (May 26, 1978), pp. A-1 and A-2.

4. *Washington Post* editorial of May 31 chided Canada for being a nation "seized of the mission of setting an example of unilateral disarmament" while huddled under the U.S. nuclear umbrella; reprinted in "Paper Needles Us on Arms," *Vancouver Sun* (May 31, 1978), p. A-1. In London, an editorial in the *Sunday Express* said of Trudeau's remarks: "Could there be any greater hypocrisy? . . . Mr. Trudeau may have won himself a few chums among the minnows at the UN. Among the world's true statesmen he rates lower than zero," in "PM 'Hypocrite,' says British paper," *Vancouver Sun* (May 29, 1978), p. A-3.

5. Trudeau, as a brilliant student of international politics and economics, had concluded years ago (after visits to Moscow and Peking) that modern history was not moving in the direction of traditional liberal democracy. In his book *The Asbestos Strike,* he saw

history as a "caravan of humanity" moving inevitably "towards the Left" and he did not intend to be left to "perish in the desert of time past." He brought this thinking with him to the East Block in 1968. (Toronto: James Lewis and Samuel, 1974), pp. 339-45.

6. *Foreign Policy For Canadians,* p. 21.

7. Philip C. Bom, *Trudeau — Truth and Consequences* (St. Catharine's: Guardian Press, 1977), p. 121.

8. Alexander Solzhenitsyn, "Warning to the Western World,"*Canadian Review* (September and October 1976).

9. George J. Keegan Jr., U.S. Air Force general who retired in 1977 as Chief of Air Force Intelligence, believes the Soviet Union is now prepared to risk nuclear war in order to emerge from the ashes with a net military advantage far beyond that of the West. Why else, he asks, are they building the world's mightiest military machine and honeycoming their nation with massive underground bunkers? He believes that the intellectual corps of western military analysts who have dominated policy making for twenty years have failed to understand that the Soviets have based their military preparations on the premise that nuclear war is more likely than not as they pursue their ideological goals throughout the world, and that their forces must be prepared to prevail in such a war and survive. Unless the West moves quickly to counterbalance burgeoning Soviet power, it "invites by inadvertence and miscalculation that which we want to avoid, global conflict." Condensed from "Soviets Can Launch, Win and Survive War Against West," *Vancouver Sun* (February 15, 1978), p. A-5.

10. Anthony Westell, *Paradox: Trudeau as Prime Minister* (Toronto: Prentice-Hall, 1972),p. 202.

11. *Defence in the 70s* (Ottawa: Information Canada, 1971).

12. James Richardson's Memo to Cabinet on Future Defence Requirements, dated November 1975.

13. Vice-Admiral R. H. Falls, "Speech to Conference of Defence Associations," January 13, 1977, mimeographed (Ottawa: DND).

14. Patrick Esmonde-White, "The Armed Forces Are a Brassy Bunch," *The Canadian Review,* p. 15.

15. Falls, "Speech to Conference of Defence Associations," January 13, 1977.

16. Ibid.

17. Peter Ward, "Baptized but not Battle Tried,"*Legion* (December 1977), p. 54.

18. Canadian Press (CP) newswire item, datelined Toronto, April 4, 1978.

19. Ibid.

20. Colonels J. E. Neelin and L. M. Pederson, "On the Effect of the Restructuring of NDHQ on the Profession of Arms in Canada," *Canadian Defence Quarterly* (CDQ) (. Summer 1974), p. 54.

21. Neelin and Pederson, "The Administrative Structure of the Canadian Armed Forces: Overly-Centralized, Overly Staff-Ridden," *CDQ,* (Autumn 1974), p. 38.

22. Neelin and Pederson, "Effect of Restructuring," *CDQ* (Summer 1974).

23. Brigadier-General, D. G. Loomis, "Forces Unification in Retrospect," mimeographed (Ottawa: DND, June 1974).

24. Armed Forces News (AFN) press release 2/68, mimeographed (Ottawa: DND).

25. "Bilingualism Policy in the CAF," *CDS Policy Directive P3/70* (Ottawa: DND, February 27, 1970).

26. Number 36 of 41 recommendations for the Public Service and the Armed Forces contained in Book 3 of The Royal Commission on Bilingualism and Biculturalism's *Final Report.* Reprinted in "Text of B&B Proposals for the Public Service," *Ottawa Journal* (December 18, 1969).

27. "Program and Plan to Increase Bilingualism and Biculturalism in the Canadian Armed Forces," issued by CDS on February 12, 1971 (Ottawa: DND).

28. Ibid, p. 3, para 13.

29. Cliff Cowan, "Bilingualism 'Threatening' Forces," *Ottawa Journal* (December 12, 1973).

30. *Defence 72* (Ottawa: Queen's Printer) gives a breakdown of language training programs. For example: "By the beginning of the academic year, 1 September, more than 5,500 servicemen were either taking language training in French or English, or were committed to take it during the 1972-73 academic year," p. 104.

31. Quoted in "Forces Remain Firm on Bilingual Policy Despite Criticisms," *Globe & Mail* (December 14, 1973).

32. Jack Best, "Unilingual English-Speaking Servicemen Concerned about Bilingualism Aims," *Ottawa Journal* (August 30, 1973).

33. DND figures.

34. "Armed Forces Bilingualism," letter to the editor, *Globe & Mail* (November 21, 1972).

35. "Bilingual Program," *Halifax Chronicle-Herald* (April 14, 1976).

36. The recommendations blueprint the final phase in the government's program to turn the forces into a bilingual "showcase," regardless of the cost in dollars or efficiency. The program is a get-tough approach to commanders in English Canada who have been slow to involve francophones in every aspect of military operations. It calls for establishment of a top-level language bureau that will coordinate, police and enforce compliance with the new initiatives, which will soon see bilingual francophones replacing anglophones in many sensitive positions at bases across the nation — including search and rescue squadrons, public information offices and *all* agencies dealing with NATO and other international agencies. The plan rings with a sense of urgency in its aim to make the forces reflect "the bilingual nature of Canada" on all fronts. The plan virtually guarantees francophone personnel many of the best jobs in the forces based primarily on linguistic ability. The plan is contained in Appendix H, "Recommendations — Special Study National Defence," in the 1977 *Annual Report* of the Commissioner of Official Languages (Ottawa: Minister of Supply and Services Canada 1978), pp. 151-169.

37. In 1972 retired Air Vice-Marshal Robert Cameron, former air attache to Washington, D.C., caused a furor in Ottawa by suggesting in a newspaper article (*Winnipeg Free Press,* April 18) that General Dextraze might have been promoted to CDS over the heads of more experienced men because he was a French-speaking Canadian, speculating that Trudeau appeared "determined to rotate the job between francophone and anglophone." Government officials hotly denied the allegation but it appears to have a grain of truth to it. In 1978, Greg Smith of Vancouver, a graduate student who had worked for Danson's office the summer before, wrote a paper on bilingualism in the forces for a notable acquaintance, Keith Spicer, former Commissioner of Official Languages. Reporting on the progress of the B&B program under Danson, Smith wrote: "Other initiatives practised by his department now include a regular rotation of linguistic groups in the selection of Chief of the Defence Staff."

38. Danson, Speech to Empire Club, Toronto, November 24, 1977, mimeographed (Ottawa: DND).

NOTES TO CHAPTER 2

1. *Defence '75* (Ottawa: Information Canada) p. 19.

2. *Defence in the 70s,* p. 28.

3. "Can Canada Enforce Its New 200-mile Fishing Conservation Zone?," *Financial Post* (February 19, 1977), p. D-14.

4. "The White Paper on Defence — Further Comment," supplement in *Maritime Affairs Bulletin 1/72,* hereafter called *M A B* (Ottawa: The Navy League of Canada).

5. Quoted from Navy League's "Viewpoint '76" workshop papers.

6. Quoted in "The Navy Under Attack," *Time* (May 8, 1978), p. 19.

7. Ibid.

8. Boyle, Speech to CDA, mimeographed (Ottawa: DND, January 14, 1977).

9. Commander W. G. Kinsman (CF ret'd), in *MAB 1/73,* article reprinted from *Proceedings of the U.S. Naval Institute* (August 1972).

10. Paul Wohl, "Soviet Navy Runs Fishing Fleet," *Christian Science Monitor* (August 18, 1976).

11. "Polar Route For Submarines," in *MAB 2/77,* p. 5; and "Soviet Subs Find Polar Route," *Vancouver Sun* (February 24, 1977), reprinted from the *Manchester Guardian.*

12. Peter Ward, "Pushed Out into the Cold," *Legion* (February 1978), p. 13.

13. Boyle, following his speech to CDA, Ottawa, January 14, 1977.

14. Falls, Speech to Canadian Club, Calgary, February 18, 1977, mimeographed (Ottawa: DND).

15. Extracted from foreword to *Jane's Fighting Ships,* 1977 edition, reprinted in *MAB 2/77,* p. 3.

16. Captain (Navy) A. L. Collier (now commander of Maritime Command), "Maritime Command Briefing for the Board of Management," in *MAB 4/71.*

17. Press Release (Ottawa: DND, February 1969).

18. Quoted in *Globe & Mail* (June 12, 1970).

19. Interviews with Commodore Caldwell and Rear-Admiral Timbrell, Ottawa, late 1976.

20. Peter Meerburg, "Details of Bonnie Fate Still Probed," *Halifax Chronicle-Herald* (April 13, 1976).

21. Donald Macdonald, "Statement to the House of Commons," November 21, 1971, intended address, mimeographed (Ottawa: DND).

22. Ibid.

23. "Significant Events," DND round-up of news, mimeographed (Ottawa: DND, July 30, 1971).

24. Quoted in "There'll Always be a Navy — Defence Chief," *Canadian Shipping* ( March 1974), p. 23.

25. Quoted in "1970 Maritime Command," *Canadian Shipping* (March 1970), p. 31.

26. Lyndon Watkins, "The Shape of Things to Come," *Canadian Shipping* (March 1974), p. 22.

27. Ibid., p. 23.

28. "Bras d'Or Battles On," *Canadian Shipping* (March 1971), p. 28.

29. Watkins, "Shape," *Canadian Shipping* (March 1974), p. 23.

30. R. H. Leir, "Let's Stop This Freeloading and Start Paying Our Own Way," *Canadian Shipping* (March 1976), p. 16.

31. "Hydrofoil in the Future," *MAB 4/77,* p. 8.

32. Leir, "Freeloading," *Canadian Shipping* (March 1976), p. 16.

33. Alex Nickerson, "Forces' Fortunes on the Upswing," *Halifax Chronicle-Herald* (November 15, 1976).

34. *MAB 1/77,* confirmed by DND sources.

35. "Statement on Defence Estimates for 1976-77 by the Honourable James Richardson to the Standing Committee on External Affairs and National Defence, March 23, 1976," mimeographed (Ottawa: DND), p. 16.

36. *MAB 1/74,* editorial.

37. *MAB 2/73.*

38. *Defence '73,* p. 36.

39. *MAB 2/73.*

40. "A Modernization and Renewal Program for the Canadian Forces," mimeographed (Ottawa: DND, October 10, 1973).

41. "Rear-Admiral Boyle's Navy," *Canadian Shipping* (March 1974), p. 18.

42. Ibid., p. 20.

43. Ibid., p. 15.

44. "Destroyers for Sale?" *MAB 2/73.*

45. *Defence '72,* p. 49.

46. Navy League's comment on Richardson's "Modernization and Renewal Program," *MAB 1/74.*

47. "A Survey of Maritime Command — 1974-75," *MAB 1/75.*

48. From the *Montreal Star* (December 23, 1974).

49. Duncan Fraser, "Canadian Forces Strength Not Adequate for Defence Policy," *Halifax Chronicle-Herald* (November 21, 1974).

50. "A Survey of Maritime Command — 1974-75," *MAB 1/75.*

51. "Maritime Command Review," *MAB 1/76.*

52. Richardson, Speech to CDA, January 17, 1975, mimeographed (Ottawa: DND).

53. Hattie Densmore, *Halifax Chronicle-Herald* (January 20, 1977).

54. Jonathon Manthorpe, "Canada Failing Military Allies, Admiral Warns," *Globe & Mail* (June 9, 1975).

55. Ibid.

56. "Statement by the Honourable James Richardson re: Press Reports on Admiral Boyle's Speech in Halifax," press release (Ottawa: DND, June 12, 1975).

57. Ron Lowman, "Warships Haven't Fired Guns in Two Years, General Says," *Toronto Star* (January 17, 1976), p. A-11.

58. *Supplement, MAB 1/77.*

59. "In Search of a New Navy," *Canadian Shipping* (May 1976), p. 14.

60. "Sea Cadet, 14, Loses Leg," *Vancouver Sun* (December 5, 1977).

61. Quoted in *Halifax Chronicle-Herald,* (April 3, 1976).

62. Dextraze, Speech to CDA, Ottawa, January 13, 1977, mimeographed (Ottawa: DND).

63. Clive Baxter, "Multi-Billion Dollar Order Book Open Again," *Financial Post* (February 19, 1977), p. D-1.

64. "Tracker Aircraft to be Updated," *Vancouver Sun* (June 17, 1976).

65. "Argus — The Long-Range Protector," *Canadian Shipping* (March 1968), p. 64.

66. "Pointed Lesson," editorial in *Halifax Chronicle-Herald* (September 9, 1975).

67. John Best, "Where Was Everyone when Gedania Slipped By?" *Ottawa Journal* (September 10, 1975).

68. Ibid.

69. "Soviet Navy 'No Ornament,'" *Halifax Chronicle-Herald* (September 5, 1975).

70. "Pursuit of Polish Yacht May Cost $400,000," editorial in *Globe & Mail* (September 12, 1975).

71. "Planes Still Seeking Elusive Polish Yacht," *London Free Press* (September 6, 1975).

72. "Have We Buried Our Navy?" *Canadian Shipping* (March 1976), pp. 12-18.

73. Falls, Speech to CDA, January 13, 1977, mimeographed (Ottawa: DND).

74. "Announcement by the Minister of National Defence on the DND Ship Replacement Program," December 22, 1977, mimeographed (Ottawa: DND) and reported in *AFN* 240/77.

75. From *Financial Post* (February 19, 1977), p. D-14.

76. Peter Ward, "Adrift in a Sea of Spending," *Legion* (March 1978), p. 12.

77. Ray Ross, reprint of his address, "Destroyer Life Extension Program," to November 2, 1977 meeting of the Canadian Shipbuilding and Ship Repairing Association, Ottawa, in *Seaport and the Shipping World* (December 1977), pp. 50-51.

78. Arnott, quoted in "New Ships for the Navy" by Brian Currie, *Financial Post* (April 15, 1978), p. 27.

79. An idea floated by Peter Ward and other naval observers and generally agreed upon by builders to be the only logical salvation for both the Navy and failing Canadian shipyards.

80. Designer's specifications and comments on Tribals' capabilities, from 1972 press release (Ottawa: DND).

81. Frank Caldwell, "Update this Destroyer and We Have a Bargain," *Canadian Shipping* (May 1976), p. 18.

82. Boyle, "In Search of a New Navy," *Canadian Shipping* (May 1976), p. 15.

83. "This Ship Has Surprised the 'Other Side' Too," *Canadian Shipping* (May 1976), pp. 15-16.

84. G. L. Edwards, Speech to the Eastern Canadian Section of the Society of Naval Architects and Marine Engineering and the Ottawa branch of the Canadian Institute of Marine Engineers; reprinted in *MAB 3/77.*

85. W. H. German, "How to Go about Modernizing the Canadian Maritime Surface Forces," *CDQ* (Summer 1976), pp. 30-31.

86. Danson, quoted in *MAB 1/77* from interview in Halifax.

87. "Canada has a lot of catching-up to do," *Financial Post* (February 19, 1977), p. D-3.

88. "Here's a Sketch of Planned New Ship," *Financial Post* (February 19, 1977), p. D-14.

89. Timbrell, "Canada's Maritime Defence Requirements," *MAB 2/77,* p. 4.

90. Ibid., pp. 2-5.

91. Peter Cale, "The Admirals Prepare for Naval Rearmament," *Canadian Shipping and Marine Engineering,* reprinted as a supplement to *MAB 2/77,* p. 4.

92. "Can Canada Enforce its New 200-mile Fishing Conservation Zone?" *Financial Post* (February 19, 1977), p. D-14.

93. "New Day Dawns for Coastal Patrol with Aurora Order," *Financial Post* (February 19, 1977), p. D-6.

94. "Can Canada Enforce," *Financial Post* (February 19, 1977).

95. Danson, speaking at a news conference in Halifax in November 1977, conjectured that it could cost $10 billion to replace the remainder of the aging fleet — twelve destroyers, three submarines and three support ships — by the year 2000. In response, the Navy League noted in *MAB 1/78* that while the sum mentioned did not represent a planning

figure and had been overblown by the press, the ships would still have to be replaced if anticipated commitments are to be met. Nevertheless, in today's dollars, the $10 billion figure does not seem unreasonable.

96. Just before he resigned, Boyle stated publicly: "We will have another world war by 1980. All the historical precedents support that view. We have the same conditions now that preceded the first two world wars — high unemployment, economic problems, a rising military might, Russia, and tariff barriers being erected all over the world." Quoted by Brian Currie, "Taught to be Honest," *Legion* (March 1978), p. 18, who added that Boyle claimed he "was asked to resign." In addition, Boyle's well known formula for world peace shows how far he was away from the government's thinking: "We must be impossible to defeat. We have to be the best killers in the world, if it comes to that. If we're recognized as the best killers, we won't ever have to do it."

97. "Experts Disagree on Coast Patrol," *The Province* (Vancouver, December 22, 1977), CP story from Ottawa.

98. Ward, "Adrift," *Legion* (March 1978), p. 12.

## Notes to Chapter 3

1. Paul Hellyer, *Address on the Canadian Forces Reorganization Act,* House of Commons, December 7, 1966 (Ottawa: Queen's Printer), p. 19.

2. *Defence '75,* p. 30.

3. Ibid.

4. Ibid., p. 31.

5. *Defence in the 70s,* p. 35.

6. Ibid.

7. Dextraze, Speech to CDA, January 16, 1976, mimeographed (Ottawa: DND).

8. Dextraze, Speech to CDA, January 13, 1977, mimeographed (Ottawa: DND).

9. Ibid., and from DND sources.

10. Cecil Merritt, "The True Requirements of Canadian Defence: A Critique of the White Paper 1971," *CDQ* (Winter 1971-72), p. 27.

11. Danson, "Revitalizing Canada's Reserves," speech to CDA, January 19, 1978, mimeographed (Ottawa: DND).

12. Ibid.

13. Ibid.

14. "The Search for a Realistic Canadian Defence Policy," a paper by Independent Research Associates, Toronto, reprinted as a supplement in *MAB 2/70*.

15. "CF-5 Boondoggle: Shameful Waste," editorial in *Toronto Star* (September 3, 1970).

16. "Jets Retired on Assembly Line," *Toronto Telegram* (August 27, 1970). Sharp also blamed government spending priorities on the mothballing of CF-5s.

17. In his 1967 memo to the Defence Council, Allard catalogued the findings from several field studies of the existing truck fleet to substantiate his case. The more than 2,000 old three-quarter-ton trucks in service had already reached the point where a minimum of $800 per vehicle was required immediately to keep them serviceable.

18. Quoted by the *Calgary Herald* (October 13, 1973).

19. Duncan Fraser, "Canadian Forces Strength Not Adequate for Defence Policy," *Halifax Chronicle-Herald* (November 21, 1974).

20. DND figures.

21. Richardson, "Modernization and Renewal" Program, October 10, 1973, mimeographed (Ottawa: DND).

22. "Budget Woes Deplete Stocks of Armed Forces' Ammunition," *Montreal Gazette* (October 18, 1975).

23. CDA Resolution Number 36, mimeographed (Ottawa: DND, 1976).

24. Transcript of panel discussion, CDA, January 16, 1976, Ottawa, mimeographed (Ottawa: DND).

25. Norman Hartley, " 'Military Midget' Declining and Troops Are Gloomy," *Globe & Mail* (October 17, 1975).

26. "Gunnery," *Armour Newsletter* (published by Combat Arms School at CFB Gagetown, June 1976), p. 4.

27. The colonel told many similar stories of training problems caused after tanks were retired. In one, a battered Volkswagen was painted up as a tank and a pole strapped to the top for authenticity. Soldiers then ran along behind the mini-panzer during simulated combat exercises.

28. *AFN 40/77* (Ottawa: DND, February 18, 1977).

29. Treasury Board Minute No. 732228, November 28, 1974.

30. Ibid.

31. John Best, "Armoured Car Deal Blocked," *Ottawa Journal* (April 1, 1976).

32. "Riot Cars Linked to Quebec," *Vancouver Sun* (March 21, 1977), a CP wire story from Toronto quoting Forrestall from interview in *Toronto Sun.*

33. "Tears Choked Back," *The Montreal Gazette* (June 15, 1970).

34. Gary Bannerman, "Kilties Frustrated by Move to Disband Highland Unit," *St. John Telegraph-Journal* (September 27, 1969).

35. "Canadians Praised by NATO," *Montreal Gazette* (December 16, 1966).

36. Leo Cadieux, *"Statement to the House of Commons,"* September 19, 1969, mimeographed (Ottawa: DND).

37. Guy Simser, "Take Everything Else, But Leave Me My Kilt," *Weekend Magazine* (August 15, 1970).

38. Duncan Fraser, "CFB Valcartier — A Good Place to Soldier," *Halifax Chronicle-Herald* (November 22, 1974).

39. DND memo, February 3, 1971.

40. *Aide Memoire* prepared for Donald Macdonald shows that while the anglophone regiments were top-heavy with NCOs, particularly corporals, the 12th was seventy-two corporals above complement. This fact was never mentioned during the debate, and DND sources say that many of the 12th's corporals were young as a result of being accelerated to that rank. This appears probable in light of the government's unexpected move to transfer in anglophone sergeants if they took French training because most corporals in the 12th would have been too inexperienced to make good senior NCOs.

41. Ibid.

42. Donald Macdonald, *"Statement to the House of Commons,"* February 4, 1971, mimeographed (Ottawa: DND).

43. *CFP 71/71.*

44. *AFN 65/76.*

45. Royal Canadian Artillery Assoication, Position Paper, for CDA conference, Ottawa, January 1976, mimeographed (Ottawa: CDA).

46. Duncan Fraser, "Canada's Army of the West Being Bled to Death," *Halifax Chronicle-Herald* (November 23, 1974).

47. *Defence '76,* p. 32.

48. Dextraze, Speech to CDA, January 13, 1977, mimeographed (Ottawa: DND).

49. *Defence '74,* p. 19.

50. In the event of nuclear war MOBCOM is tasked to provide regional commanders with troops trained and disciplined to undertake post-nuclear strike responsibilities in Canada. "These would include warning the public of fallout, re-entry to a nuclear disaster area, and assistance to the civilian population such as providing first aid, feeding and other emergency service." From *Defence '74,* p. 19.

51. John Gellner, quoted in *Globe & Mail* (August 25, 1971).

52. Gellner, quoted in *Globe & Mail* (October 26, 1973).

53. Merritt, "True Requirements," *CDQ* (Winter 71/72), p. 27.

54. John Gellner has noted several times that Ottawa's reluctance to spend a few million to maintain a civil defence agency of any size has its roots in semantics. Richardson cut civil defence spending because he was convinced the provinces had used some of the funds given to them for peacetime emergencies, such as fires and floods. Trouble is, believes Gellner, that regardless of what type of disaster befalls, it is unwise to allow the nation's only civil disaster agency to perish because of the

inability of Ottawa and the provinces to work out an equitable cost-sharing formula.

55. Peter Silverman, "Lack of Troops Pinches Mobile Command, Too," *Financial Post* (February 19, 1977), p. D-18.

56. Colonel Strome Galloway, "Defence: The Great Canadian Fairy Tale," *The British Army Journal* (London, 1972), p. 424.

57. "Speed Troop Movement, NATO Asks U.S., Britain, Canada," *Globe & Mail* (July 2, 1976), Reuter story from Brussels.

58. Silverman, "Lack of Troops," *Financial Post* (February 19, 1977).

59. "Forces Stretched to Limit, Defence Official Declares," *Toronto Star* (July 7, 1975).

60. *Report 30,* "Standing Committee on External Affairs and National Defence (Ottawa: Queen's Printer, November 25, 1975), pp. 30:12-13.

61. Nicholas Stethem, "My War with the Army," *Maclean's* (March 1975), p. 60.

62. "Canada sends 80 to Lebanon," *Vancouver Sun* (April 17, 1978). CP story from Kamloops quoting Jamieson after speech at fund-raising dinner for Environment Minister Len Marchand.

63. Stethem, "My War," *Maclean's* (March 1975), p. 60.

64. Richardson, "Discussion on Peacekeeping Resolution —November 14, 1973," House of Commons, mimeographed (Ottawa: DND).

65. *Defence '75,* p. 32.

66. *Defence '74,* p. 19.

67. Dextraze, Speech to CDA, January 13, 1977, mimeographed (Ottawa: DND).

68. Robert Lewis, "The Unhappy Warrior," *Maclean's* (July 24, 1978), p. 17.

69. *Edmonton Journal* (January 9, 1976), p. 2.

70. Dextraze, Speech to CDA, January 13, 1977.

71. Duncan Fraser, "Canada's Airborne Regiment under Attack," *Halifax Mail-Star* (June 21, 1976).

72. Dick Brown, "Hanging Tough," *Quest* (May 1978), pp. 10-22.

73. Ibid.

74. "Inflation-Hit Armed Forces Tightening Belts," *Montreal Gazette* (October 22, 1974).

75. Painchaud's remarks reprinted in "Men Bitter at Losing 'Gutsy' Colonel," *Vancouver Province* (July 14, 1978), p. 7.

76. McKinnon expressed opinion that Danson's comments in *Legion* were designed to test reaction to planned move, in "Fired Colonel's Former Troops Bitter over Danson's Reaction," *Vancouver Sun* (July 14, 1978), p. A-10. The regiment and DND sources had long expected the government to announce it would disband the airborne after the move east.

77. Ibid.

78. Ibid.

79. Ibid.

80. Ibid.

## NOTES TO CHAPTER 4

1. Dr. G. R. Lindsey, "A Useful New Role for the Canadian Forces in Europe," *CDQ* (Summer 1974), p. 28.

2. Jeffrey Record, summary of his Brookings' Institute study, in *Canadian Military Journal* (Winter 1976), p. 1.

3. Colin Gray, *Canadian Defence Priorities: A Question of Relevance* (Toronto: Clark, Irwin & Co., 1972), p. 97.

4. "Next Six Years Crucial for NATO," *Ottawa Journal* (October 18, 1969).

5. Bob Gilmour, "Across the Border, the Threat Keeps Growing," *Edmonton Journal* (November 5, 1976), p. 27.

6. Leonard Bertin, "Clearly, We Have a Lot to Learn," *Kingston Whig-Standard* (October 22, 1976).

7. Dextraze, Speech to CDA, Ottawa, January 16, 1976.

8. Ibid.

9. *Toronto Star* (August 8, 1972).

10. Robert MacDonald, "NATO Troops Tops, but Our Equipment over the Hill," *Toronto Sun* (October 26, 1975).

11. DND figures.

12. DND public relations handout, undated.

13. Bertin, "A Look at Strategies and Weapons along the Curtain," *Kingston Whig-Standard* (October 18, 1976).

14. Nicholas Stethem, "My War with the Army," *Maclean's* (March 1975), p. 56.

15. "Annex B" to VCDS "Memorandum to the Defence Management Committee (DMC)," on "Procurement of a Direct Fire Support Vehicle," February 17, 1972, Ottawa.

16. Captain D. J. Thompson, "The Artillery of the Canadian Forces: The Need for Organizational and Material Modernization," *CDQ* (Summer 1976), p. 18.

17. Ibid.

18. John Gellner, "The Lean Years Haunt the Fattening-Up Plan," *Globe & Mail* (October 16, 1973).

19. *Defence '76,* p. 43.

20. *Toronto Sun* (August 30, 1972).

21. Ibid.

22. John Gellner, "Ottawa Regains Faith in NATO," *Globe & Mail* (October 24, 1975).

23. DND figures.

24. Dextraze, 1973 memo indicating cost for battlefield helicopters could reach $400 million.

25. Claude Adams, "They Sneak and Peek," *Montreal Star* (August 7, 1976).

26. DND public relations handout, undated.

27. Anthony Westell, *Paradox: Trudeau as Prime Minister,* (Toronto: Prentice-Hall, 1972), p. 202.

28. Gray, *Canadian Defence Priorities,* p. 97.

29. Robert Cameron, "Anti-Tank Edict Unreasonable," *Halifax Chronicle-Herald* (May 31, 1974).

30. "Why Tanks Shouldn't Be Scrapped," *Globe & Mail* December 13, 1973).

31. Dextraze, "Aide-memoire for discussion of Scorpion/Centurion situation," January 8, 1973, Ottawa.

32. Cadieux, "Statement to the House of Commons," September 19, 1969, mimeographed (Ottawa: DND).

33. *Defence in the 70s,* p. 35.

34. Gray, *Canadian Defence Priorities,* p. 97.

35. DND draft press release dated April 1971.

36. "Benson Bargains for Scorpion Tanks," *Montreal Star* (July 26, 1972).

37. Internal DND document on Scorpion deployment.

38. Dextraze, "Aide-memoire," January 8, 1973, Ottawa.

39. Ibid.

40. MacDonald, *Toronto Sun* (July 16, 1975).

41. MacDonald, *Toronto Sun* (October 26, 1975).

42. Ibid.

43. Richardson, Speech to The Conference of Honorary Colonels and Lieutenant-Colonels of the Militia and Air Reserve, Ottawa, November 15, 1975, mimeographed (Ottawa: DND).

44. Letter to the Editor, *Ottawa Citizen* (April 16, 1977).

45. " 'Super Tank' Armour Unveiled by Britain," *Ottawa Journal* (June 18, 1976).

46. Dextraze, Speech to CDA, Ottawa, January 13, 1977.

47. Lindsey, "Useful New Role," *CDQ* (Summer 1974), p. 31.

48. Trudeau, quoted in "PM Backs Arms Buildup as NATO Survival Need," *Vancouver Sun* (May 3, 1978), pp. A-1 to A-2.

49. Ibid.

50. "Defence Budget Won't Rise, PM Says," *Vancouver Sun* (June 2, 1978), CP wire story from Ottawa.

### NOTES TO CHAPTER 5

1. *Defence in the 70s,* p. 35.

2. Margaret MacMillan, "NORAD Mission Is a Thing of the Past, Critics Say," *Toronto Star* (June 3, 1975). Professor Clarkson is quoted from 1972 interview.

3. Cameron, "NORAD's Value to Canada," *Regina Leader-Post* (June 4, 1973).

4. Gellner, letter to the editor, *Globe & Mail* (September 15, 1972).

5. Memo to James Richardson from ADM Sylvain Cloutier, March 27, 1975.

6. "Cuts in Military Spending 'Hurts'," *Ottawa Citizen* (October 24, 1974).

7. Clive Baxter, "Point of No Return Nears on $2 Billion Aerospace Crunch," *Financial Post* (July 12, 1975).

8. *Defence '75,* p. 42.

9. "New Equipment to be Sought to Modernize NORAD Radar," *Financial Post* (February 19, 1977), p. D-4.

10. Ibid.

11. Ibid.

12. House of Commons, *Minutes of Proceedings and Evidence of the Standing Committee on External Affairs and National Defence* (Ottawa: Queen's Printer, April 22, 1975), p. 14:31.

13. Ibid., p. 14:18.

14. Dextraze, Speech to CDA, January 13, 1977.

15. Lieutenant-General William Carr, "Components of a Modernized Aerospace Defence System," *CDQ* (Summer 1974), p. 24.

16. Lieutenant-General William Carr, "The New Fighter Aircraft: Operational Requirements and Desirable Characteristics," *CDQ* (Summer 1976), pp. 16-17.

17. Hugh Quigley, "Pilot Training in the CAF," *Canadian Aviation* (August 1976), p. 38.

18. Ibid.

19. Ibid., p. 39.

20. Ibid.

21. Ibid.

22. *AFN 55/77,* March 18, 1977, DIS.

23. House of Commons, *Standing Committee Report,* p. 14:11.

24. Gellner, "Time to Put Sinews into National Defence," *Reader's Digest* (November 1976).

25. DND figures.

26. *AFN 55/77.*

27. "Used Warplanes Offered," *Globe & Mail* (November 25, 1976) and interview with McKinnon.

28. Clive Baxter, "Cabinet Agrees to Tackle its $2 Billion Flying Headache," *Financial Post* (September 20, 1975), p. 4.

29. Carr, see *CDQ* articles in Summer 1975, 1976.

30. Baxter, "Cabinet Agrees," *Financial Post* (September 20, 1975).

31. "Which of These Fighters Is Best for Canada," *Financial Post* (September 20, 1975), p. 4.

32. Ibid.

33. Frederick Page, quoted in Munich interview, "Panavia Tornado, Profile of a Contender," *Financial Post* (April 15, 1978), p. 11.

# INDEX